MW00977608

THE SCRIBAL ANOINTING

"SCRIBES INSTRUCTED IN THE KINGDOM OF HEAVEN"

THERESA HARVARD JOHNSON

Revised & Expanded Edition

Copyright © 2007, 2016 by Theresa Harvard Johnson
All Rights Reserved. No part of this publication may be reproduced, stored in a retrieval system or transmitted in any form or by any means electronic, mechanical, photocopying, recording or otherwise, without prior written permission of the publisher.

Third Printing, 2016

ISBN-13: 978-1535082228
ISBN-10: 1535082224

Theresa Harvard Johnson
950 Eagles Landing Parkway, #302
Stockbridge, Georgia 30281

Scripture quotations, unless otherwise indicated, are taken from the New King James Version®. Copyright © 1982 by Thomas Nelson, Inc. Used by permission. All rights reserved.

Scripture quotations marked (AMP) are taken from the *Amplified Bible*, Copyright © 1954, 1958, 1962, 1964, 1965, 1987 by The Lockman Foundation. Used by permission.

Scripture quotations are taken from the Holy Bible, New Living Translation, copyright ©1996, 2004, 2007, 2013, 2015 by Tyndale House Foundation. Used by permission of Tyndale House Publishers, Inc., Carol Stream, Illinois 60188. All rights reserved.

Scripture taken from the New King James Version®. Copyright © 1982 by Thomas Nelson. Used by permission. All rights reserved.

Printed in the United States of America.

If you purchased this book without a cover, you should be aware that this book is stolen property. It is reported as "unsold and destroyed" to the publisher and neither the author, or publisher has received any payment for this stripped book.

Dedication

To every prophetic scribe in search of their identity in Christ…

Declaration

"Every believer should use whatever gift he has received to serve others, faithfully administering God's grace in its various forms. If anyone speaks, he should do it as one speaking the very words of God. If anyone serves, he should do it with the strength God provides, so that in all things God may be praised through Jesus Christ. To him be the glory and the power forever and ever."

~ 1 Peter 4:10-11

Table of Contents

FROM THE AUTHOR

It's hard to believe that 13 years have passed since the Lord began unfolding the in-depth revelation of The Scribal Anointing® into my heart. I was studying about biblical scribes and teaching nuggets of what I had learned in 2003, but never imagined that all that study would come to a head one evening in 2005 as a I read the book of Ezra in preparation for a prophetic writing conference.

In the middle of my study, I heard the Lord say: *"There is a revival of the Scribal Anointing upon the land. I, beloved, am revealing myself to my people through my creative word. They will write, spread the good news and testify with passion before men. I will release them as secret weapons in these last days."* Little did I know that this would set the course for the ministry entrusted to me today.

My spirit leapt with excitement! I began praising God and thanking him for sharing his prophetic insight concerning this gift and calling. I gloried in God's revelation that day as I remembered that Ezra, the priest, was the only scribe in and of the bible whom the scriptures referred to plainly as a scribe who *"prepared and set his heart to seek the law of the Lord – to teach it and to walk in its statutes"* and a scribe *"of the instructions of the Kingdom of God"* (**Ezra 7:10, 12**).

This may not seem like a ground-breaking revelation to some, but for me – it changed everything! It shifted the evangelistic ministry I had been leading across Atlanta and neighboring states into a completely new place of spiritual existence.... and ultimately, led me to you today! There's something to be said about not despising small beginnings.

The scribes we've grown familiar with as believers of Christ had a negative reputation when it came to the Kingdom of God. They were only remembered for the chaos and confusion that followed them in the New Covenant. Holy Spirit revealed to me that this was only part of their story. Through a great deal of intensive study, I learned that the scribes God chose in the beginning were, in fact, honorable – and worthy of that honor. As the old folks would say, it only takes one rotten able to spoil the entire bunch. But guess what, this is only a fraction of the story.

It was in this place of KNOWING that there was greater to draw from scribes of the Bible that the Lord began to open up **Matthew 13:52** in the King James Version of the Bible. The ultimate key to this parable was hidden in simply knowing that Christ, our deliverer, was referring to Ezra when He declared: *"Therefore every scribe instructed concerning the Kingdom of Heaven is like a householder who brings out of his treasure things new and old."*

For serious writers who live to glorify Christ, I believe this teaching is transformational. Father has been using this book, "The Scribal Anointing: Scribes Instructed in the Kingdom of Heaven," to bring a total and complete metamorphosis into the heart of the prophetic writer and prophetic scribe in this season. Father is using this teaching to give them a strong, biblical identity that causes them to really consider what they publish in the earth through their lives and scribal ministries. He is also using this teaching to help us develop a lifestyle that lines up with **John 14:15**.

Present day "prophetic" scribes are the Solomons of the 21st Century (2 Chronicles 1:11-12).

For the first time in over a decade, I am fully revising, *The Scribal Anointing: Scribes Instructed in the Kingdom of Heaven*. To say it is long overdue for an extensive overhaul is an understatement! First and foremost, my revelation of the scribe has grown extensively to say the least. Secondly, there's quite a bit of content that needs updating, correcting, adding to and expounded upon. I am a person who believes in starting with what you have… and GROWING from that place unashamedly. But over time, I have matured, grown in my understanding of the Word, connected some much needed dots and have a broader apostolic grasp of this revelation.

I also stand equipped to defend it.

Listen, this book is written solely based on Holy Spirit inspiration… and originally, my resources and understanding of publishing was extremely limited. I learned to do everything from scratch -- from formatting the pages and designing the cover, to figuring out how to print the first copy myself. Some of you know what I mean. When we know better, we learn to do better! With that said, this revision is also necessary because I needed to update the look and feel for the book to fit the 21st century renewal that is upon us. I needed to provide citations, proper attribution and supporting reference materials where needed.

At the end of the day, I pray that this revised and expanded edition will deeply touch your heart, AND bring greater clarity concerning the ministry of the scribe. Some of my original sources, however, are no longer in print or accessible via the web. I believe that what is provided is sufficient for our purposes here.

I prophesy today that you will unlock your destiny, clarify your purpose and get understanding like never before concerning your calling as a prophetic scribe of the King. I declare that you will fulfill the ministry God has entrusted to you for HIS GLORY! You and I have spent years allowing the systems of this world to tell us who we are in the midst of our gifts and callings. Just think about how many years you spent moving through prekindergarten, kindergarten, elementary, middle and high school.

And for those who went on to pursue secondary degrees, an additional five to 10 years can be added! I know… as this is my testimony. Whether we realize it or not, everything we learned in academia or any other continuing education initiatives have shaped who we have come to see ourselves as in the writing and scribal arenas.

Only Holy Spirit can take all that we have learned and put it in a proper, Kingdom perspective. I set my foundation for teaching you about the ministry of the prophetic scribe and the prophetic writer on **Philippians 3:8-10 NKJV**. It reads, *"…I also count all things loss for the excellence of the knowledge of Christ Jesus my Lord, for whom I have suffered the loss of all things, and count them as rubbish, that I may gain Christ and be found in Him, not having my own righteousness, which is from the law, but that which is through faith in Christ, the righteousness which is from God by faith; that I may know Him and the power of His resurrection, and the fellowship of His sufferings, being conformed to His death…"*

My heart for Christ is fierce, intense. His sacrifice and calling *is not* casual for me. I pray that it is not casual for you either. I believe firmly in living my life – and teaching others to live their lives – from a place of immersion in the midst of their faith and belief. In this day and time that is old-school thinking according to some. So as you move through this book, I want to encourage you to keep this insight ever present before you. As you read, learn and grow, don't keep the areas that resonate deeply within your soul to yourself. Purchase a printed copy of this book or eBook for a friend. This is not only an opportunity to support me in the midst of this journey to reach millions of believers with this message, but an opportunity for YOU to change lives with what you have learned.

We are living in the TIME of the 21st Century prophetic scribe! It is truly our SEASON to arise and take our rightful places in the Kingdom – as creatives, administrators and instructors. We have the responsibility of continuing the work of the scribe… ensuring that the message of the Gospel and the Work of Holy Spirit in the earth is protected, preserved for generations to come. Earnestly, we cannot do this if we fail to truly comprehend who we are in Christ. Our role in this dispensation of the Gospel is critical. By the time you complete this book and the workbook, *The Scribal Companion*, I pray that you will have come to know this as well. Surely, we are walking in a very critical span of time for the congregation. The avenues and methods of communication are global and instant. We have wireless technologies, endless possibilities through the web and an ever changing landscape of digital devices and services at our disposal. Just this year, drones began delivering mail in place of mail delivery services in some areas. In addition, a tremendous amount of focus is being placed on accessing and dispensing information quickly and accurately in every imaginable aspect of our lives. I have learned to say that the days of George Jetson, a cartoon from the 1970s, are literally upon us!

What does this mean? It means we have so many new, affordable avenues to present God's heart to His people. Doors have opened for the prophetic scribe today that were previously closed. No longer are we at the mercy of agents, publishers or elite groups of scholars who dictate what is worth printing and what is not. This is not a negative pun, but it speaks to the liberty that has been set before us. Consider this truth: At no time in HISTORY has an ordinary man or woman been able to publish, produce or promote the way we can today. No longer are we at the sole mercy of marketing agencies and advertisers who only take certain clients or literary genres. Truly, we are in a new era and God is speaking, guiding, and commanding so many of us to move.

My role in this is to provide the kind of guidance concerning "scribal identity" that will allow us to move effortlessly and effectively in the Spirit. We have been commanded to "get understanding" – and we are not talking about knowledge alone, but personal revelation concerning what God wants from our surrendered lives.!

I pray that as you read this book, you will do so with an open heart, an open mind and the posture of a student – not a critic. While I have provided details on what scribal ministry is, we go into a greater depth and intensity at our workshops and schools of ministry. Scribal ministry is extremely broad and wide! I pray that you seek to hear the heart of God concerning your own purpose, destiny… and especially your identity as a prophetic scribe. Then consider how your unique scribal walk could impact nations. I pray that you choose to love God the way scripture reveals! I pray that you serve Him in the pattern of Christ, totally abandoning your own will for His!

I pray that you experience a scribal awakening in your heart – one that is limitless, unashamed and bold! I pray that His trumpet blows purely through you fulfilling **Isaiah 61** in present day. I pray that the words God has inspired permeates your heart and transforms your soul!

I urge you, as my brothers and sisters in the Lord, to always remember that Jesus Christ *did not* come to entertain you but to set the captives free.

Embracing Immersion,

Theresa Harvard Johnson
Voices of Christ Apostolic-Prophetic School of the Scribe

PART I: FOUNDATION BUILDING

"According to the grace of God which was given to me, as a wise master builder I have laid the foundation, and another builds on it. But let each one take heed how he builds on it. For no other foundation can anyone lay than that which is laid, which is Jesus Christ."
~ **1 Corinthians 3:10-11**

SETTING THE STAGE

Before jumping directly into this teaching, there are several things that must be cleared up or clarified to help put this book, *"The Scribal Anointing: Scribes Instructed in the Kingdom of Heaven,"* in proper context. I **strongly** suggest you review this section before moving forward.

(1) **The Old Covenant.** I spend a great deal of time uncovering the ministry of the prophetic scribe through the Old Covenant. The reason behind this is simple: The identity and ministry of the scribe is unveiled in detail in the Old Covenant. The New Covenant simply does not have the vivid examples, historical background and scriptural context that we can tap into here. In addition, it provides us with a way to – at least to some degree – follow the evolution of the scribe from the time they are first introduced from a ministry perspective into the time of the apostles.

(2) **We begin with Moses.** Surely, I could talk about the history of scribes from an ancient perspective of Mesopotamia in the Middle East to Moses, David and Ezra. Unfortunately, this would be a scholarly undertaking that, quite frankly has already been done, and does not fit within the scope of our purpose here. Rather, our journey begins when scribes were first "officially set in office" as ministers and governors over the children of Israel. Because our focus is our *prophetic* lineage, we start at a point when scribes first prophesied and were positioned as leaders over the people. The Scribal Anointing has its roots in "this" history. It's that simple.

(3) **Jewish history.** I will cover quite a bit of information pertaining to Jewish history with you in the opening of the book. The bottom line is that we cannot dig into understanding the ministry of the scribe without discussing Jewish customs, life and other historical data. The goal is not to turn toward any type of movement. What is shared helps us put the scriptures, the context of the scribe and scribal ministry in its proper place. I believe that when we can decipher scripture in a historical context as well as the spiritual that we can better understand what the biblical authors are saying to us in present day.

(4) **About scribes.** The history of biblical scribes is intense. While we have historical information on their roles in antiquity, scholars battle over their origin, rise and even their transition. As a result, there are many conflicting accounts relating to various aspects of their lives and ministries as it pertains to the children of Israel. In fact, the scribes that walked with Moses all but vanished from history. This, however, does not mean that those functions ceased to exist or that the work stopped. It simply means that the seeds planted during that time entered a transition that paved the way for varying scribal resurrections through the Bible – including those in the reign of David, the reformation brought forth through Ezra and what we see emerge in the New Covenant. **My point is simple:** This book is not about outlining all of those twists and turns. There are many academic texts that can help you sort that out if this is your interest. In the footnotes and bibliography, you will find clues that will help you do just that if this is your desire. Our goal here is to

reveal the "seeds" that have given way to the watering of scribal ministry today from a prophetic perspective. That we can see ourselves being revealed through God's Word.

(5) **Things lost.** When I began writing this book over a decade ago, I was a new author and I was driven to get this book published. There was a great deal I did not know. I drew from so many sources. Back then, I didn't understand the importance of building a strong bibliography. Unfortunately, several drive failures and lost-printed-files-later... I could not find some of my original notes and citations. So, I have had to go back and literally re-research some of the key areas of the text using my own scribal library (which is extensive now), seminary graduate training and online research to properly cite this text. Remember, this is a revised and expanded edition. As a result, the sources will range from the last three or four years to as much as a decade ago. We live and we learn.

(6) **Revelation.** Outside of historical facts and scriptural evidence, this book is based entirely on a prophetic revelation I received directly from the Lord concerning the ministry of the prophetic scribe. In other words, Holy Spirit unlocked this book within me. The tying together of the varying aspects of this book are a part of that revelation – and is in no way tied to any other group, ministry, teaching, camp, etc. Its intent is simple: To clearly build the "spiritual" identity of the present day scribe; and to cause them to walk out their ministries in faithfulness and loyalty to God over man.

These six points should bring some clarity to those who may have some specific questions about why certain information was or was not included. As with all present day, prophetic writings, this message will surely connect with those who have an ear to hear what God is continuing to unveil about the 21st century prophetic scribe. Now, let's begin this journey together.

A BRIEF BIBLICAL HISTORY OF THE SCRIBE

Scribes of Old

Let's start with the obvious question, "What is a scribe?" By contemporary definitions a scribe is defined as a serious, passionate writer, journalist, editor or teacher. Considering the day and time in which we live and the varying literary gifts that are bursting forth in this season, this definition is quite appropriate for the general population. It doesn't, however, accurately convey who we are from a biblical perspective – especially those who believe they are called to be a prophetic scribe.

The term "scribe" as translated in its original Hebrew text is סָפַר (caphar), pronounced saw-far.[1] It literally means to count, to recount or to number. As a noun, it means enumerator, muster-officer, *secretary or scribe*.[2] When the scribes copied Torah (specifically the first five books of the Bible also known as the Law of Moses or Mosaic Law), they counted each "holy" letter as they wrote it for accuracy and precision.[3] Copying the law was a specific task generally assigned to a type of master scribe called a *sofer*. These scribes were devout in their service to God, and received special training in their profession.[4]

Copying the Torah was a time consuming, costly and laborious process.[5] If one mistake was made the entire scroll could be destroyed. The beauty of this knowledge is that it reveals just how serious the profession, art and ministry of the scribe was and is in Jewish culture. Scribes were focused on precision and accuracy. In addition, patience was a critical attribute for all scribes – but particularly for the sofer, as it could take up to one year for a single Torah scroll to be completed.[6]

> **FACT:** The profession of the scribe was indispensable to the Jewish community, and according to the Talmud a scholar should not dwell in a town where there is no scribe.[7]

---

[1] The meaning of "scribe" is taken from "Strong's Definitions," a collection of the unique Greek and Hebrew words and their definitions from the Old and New Testament, organized by Dr. James Strong in 1890. This definition was retrieved online at Blue Letter Bible, https://goo.gl/P1w7ZO.

[2] Ibid.

[3] Michal Shekel. "The Making of a Torah Scroll," My Jewish Learning, http://www.myjewishlearning.com/article/torah-scroll/

[4] Ibid.

[5] Catherine Hezser, *Jewish Literacy in Roman Palestine* (Tubingen:2001), 480.

[6] Torah Scroll Facts, Chabad.org, http://www.chabad.org/library/howto/wizard_cdo/aid/351655/jewish/Torah-Scroll-Facts.htm

[7] Jewish Virtual Library, Encyclopedia Judaica: Scribe, (The Gale Group: 2008), http://www.jewishvirtuallibrary.org/jsource/judaica/ejud_0002_0018_0_17895.html

Scribes of old were not only sofers but highly educated men who worked professionally as copyists, clerks, recorders, secretaries, lawyers, judges and record keepers among many other functions.[8]

They were administrators who had been trained from their youth to *expertly* interpret, teach and copy the Law of Moses. [9] Every scribe was taught by a master scribe in what has come to be referenced as a scribe school or school of the scribe. This school did not necessarily start out as a formal institution as we recognize them to be today. Rather, the environment may have involved family like guilds[10] or groups, and then evolved into other forms later in history. It is also important to note that scribes began their training as young as five years old,[11] some accounts infer that training could have begun as young as age 4.

Philip R. Davies states that "in Judah and elsewhere in the ancient Near East, the scribes can be identified as the 'intellectuals' or 'sages' or 'as the wise,' and especially responsible for wisdom literature." [12] **Get this, scribes were the beginning of a literary revolution in Judah!** These extraordinary men AND WOMEN expanded their interests to not only preserve and protect the Word of God, but to ultimately preserve and protect the history of their culture and their people. It took a great deal of digging to begin to uncover facts about women who were trained in scribe schools, although antiquity does not traditionally acknowledge them. But that's another book! The legacy of the scribe reveals that scribes developed a reservoir of literary material, their own style of composition and were experts in the use of the pen and book.[13] In many ways, they were among the first people to organize writing as a profession and as a discipline. Davies stated:

---

[8]Ibid.

[9]Ibid.

[10]Note: As in neighboring lands, the Israelite scribe learned his profession in family-like guilds (cf. "the families of scribes who inhabited Jabez," I Chron. 2:5). A 15th century B.C.E. text does indicate the existence of scribal schools in Canaan proper. It is a letter written by a teacher to a student's father living in Shechem asking for the long overdue tuition fee that could be paid in kind. The teacher describes his relationship to his students as that of a parent. Jewish Virtual Library, Scribes, http://www.jewishvirtuallibrary.org/jsource/judaica/ejud_0002_0018_0_17895.html

[11]Bible Scholar Online, *Study Shows Jesus as Rabbi,* http://www.biblescholars.org/2013/05/study-shows-jesus-as-rabbi.html

[12]Philip R. Davies, *Scribes and Schools: The Canonization of the Hebrew Scriptures,* (Kentucky, Westminster John Knox Press: 1998), 74.

[13]Ibid, 75.

"The scribal duties, as has been seen, traditionally embraced a range of activities, amounting to a good deal of ideological control: archiving (possession and control of the present), historiography (possession and control of the past), didactic writing (maintenance of social values among the elite), and predictive writing (possession and control of the future). The traditional ethos of the scribal class itself generated works of instruction, speculation on the meaning of life, social ethics, cosmology and manticism. Hence in Judah, as elsewhere in the ancient near-east, the scribes can be identified as 'intellectuals,' or as 'sages,' or as 'the wise,' and especially responsible for wisdom literature.[14]"

Yes, I know this sounds over the top scholarly... and a tad bit on the too much information side. But what I want you to see here is the LEVEL of contribution scribes had in antiquity and to consider that they are still maintaining those postures today – inside and outside of the congregation. Davie's perspective here is noteworthy if, for no other reason than to understand the kind of impact we have – as a scribal nation – in the earth today. So you see, we are talking about a vast and broad perspective here. Our potential as a scribal nation expands every single time we gain greater insight and understanding into who we are within the context of our biblical history and especially as it relates to our spiritual heritage.

These scribes were not a ragtag group of writers, researchers and teachers! They memorized the law, taught it to those assigned to them, raised up other scribes and passed down customs, traditions and varying beliefs that were pertinent to the generations. They served kings, priests, prophets and apostles throughout biblical history on various accountability levels; but their most prized roles were protecting the law, which we will discuss briefly later; as well as interpreting and teaching the Word. That place of "interpretation" was not solely about providing comprehension in the sense of student learning; but it referred to interpreting the law as it related to customs and legal matters – as in a court of law or in application to legislation that governed a nation.

Scribes were classed in three areas: Temple scribes, royal scribes and scribes by profession. Those who worked in the temple or handled temple affairs could be classed as temple scribes. The sofer scribe, to whom we are most closely linked as prophetic writers, would be assigned to the temple or temple affairs, as would secretaries, treasurers, archivists, etc. Kings would employ royal scribes, who were trained under and assigned to the king's court (administration) and military forces. Their roles and responsibilities mirror government entities heavily... and probably provide a broader view of the types of roles scribes might hold. There is extensive insight on the activity of royal scribes during the reign of King David and King Solomon.

---

[14]Ibid, 74.

In service to kings, many of them held high ranking positions. Some scribes could also be hired out for professional service to write contracts and other important documents like marriage or divorce decrees. They served in the capacity we might recognize from a notary or magistrate of some kind. Also, it was not uncommon for scribes to be financially compensated for services rendered – especially as it related to notary services and writing divorce decrees.[15] For those who believe they cannot charge for the services they provide, please know that this was common in antiquity. The scribal call was clearly tied to ministry; but it was also a business – the livelihood of the come scribes at that time. Scribes also served as census takers, judges, heralds, etc. They were privy to all the goings-on in the Kingdom. In some instances, they had a greater level of influence than kings or high priests. Ironically, they often served as interim successors when kings died or were otherwise deposed.[16] This, as you can imagine, wasn't always positive.

    FACT: Scribes used a special ink, paper, pens or styluses when copying the law.

How did scribes gain all of this influence among the Hebrew people anyway? How did they become so intricately immersed in Kingdom culture – to a point where the Kingdom literally depended on them for its survival? From my perspective, the answer to this question can betraced back to the priesthood of Moses. They held positions of authority, power and influence that was necessary to keep order, propel the message of Torah and to maintain Israel's traditions. The scribal pattern revealed through Moses is where the legacy began.

Let's take a closer look at the role scribes had with Moses and the people.

In **Numbers 11:14-17** God instructed Moses to create an administrative council to assist him with managing the children of Israel whom he shepherded. This administrative council's **primary function** was _to relieve Moses of many of the administrative burdens associated with pasturing or leading God's people._ Scribes held key positions on this council which was called the Sanhedrin, which means the "great council" or "great assembly."[17] At one time, it was considered the highest _judiciary_ and _ecclesiastical_ council of the first century.

The scripture begins with Moses complaint to God, followed by God's response: **_"I am not able to bear all these people alone, because the burden is too heavy for me._** _If You treat me like this, please kill me here and now – if I have found favor in Your sight – and do not let me see my wretchedness! So the LORD said to Moses:_ **Gather to Me _seventy men of the elders of Israel,_ whom you know to be _the elders of the people and officers over them;_ bring them to the tabernacle of meeting, that they may stand there with you.** _Then I will come down and talk with you there. I will take of the Spirit that is upon you and will put the same upon them; and they shall bear the burden of the people with you, that you may not bear it yourself alone."_

---

[15]Jewish Virtual Library, Encyclopedia Judaica, http://www.jewishvirtuallibrary.org/jsource/judaica/ejud_0002_0018_0_17895.html

[16]Davies, 78.

[17]The Sanhedrin, Recent Attempt to Re-establish the Sanhedrin in Eretz Yisroel, http://www.thesanhedrin.org/en/index.php/Historical_Overview

Moses chose 70 elders to sit on this council according to the instructions given to him by God. Including himself, there were 71. To put this in perspective, we need to consider that Moses probably had tens of thousands in his company. According to **Exodus 12:36**, there were approximately 600,000 people on foot traveling with him. This number is hotly debated from a scholarly perspective in which some theologians' site mistranslation of scripture or conflicts with other censuses. What we do know, however, is that the number was likely in the thousands. Moses really did have a nation of people with him. It wasn't small, and it was an enormous burden for one man. When examining the role these elders played amid the people, it should not surprise us that those "seventy" consisted of one-third each of chief priests, elders and scribes **(Mark 15:1)**. The odd number existed so that there would never be a tie on matters that involved voting.

In the Strong's Concordance, the word "officer" as it is used in **Numbers 11** is specifically translated "scribe, overseer, ruler" in Hebrew. It literally means the following:

> **OFFICER | Strong's H7860**
> שֹׁטֵר active participle of an otherwise unused root probably meaning to write; properly, **a scribe,** i.e. (by analogy or implication) an official superintendent or magistrate: — officer, overseer, ruler.

Listen, I remember when Father instructed me to exegete this passage. I had no idea what I would uncover or that Moses' Great Council had strong scribal connections. **Numbers 11:15-16** clearly shows that **all of those chosen were elders and all of those chosen were scribes**. For me this means one thing: Moses had a kicking team of scribes! Further, it shows that even though they were trained scribes… some of them held positions as priests, others served in the overseeing capacity of elders, and others fulfilled their role in varying capacities as trained scribes. Another meaning associated with the Sanhedrin's meaning was "a council chamber," as in a supreme council that organized to assess weighty matters of the Kingdom.[18] Can you imagine the level of knowledge and wisdom Moses now had at his disposal? The scripture clearly says to choose those who are "officers *and* elders over the people" not "officers or elders." Also note that these were GOVERNMENTAL scribes or foundation setting scribes. The word "officer" indicates that they were "scribal rulers or scribal officers." People of God, we need to realize that scribes were foundational to the first official "God-centered" government ever formed and set over his people for corporate administrative and ministerial affairs. It's kind of ironic, at least in my opinion, that many people in the midst of the congregation still separate administration from the work of ministry… and view it as a non-spiritual activity. The thing is, apostolic order always comes before the prophetic. But that's another story.

To further support this, take a look at these comments from Cameron Freeman. He writes:

---

[18]Hitchcock, Roswell D. "Entry for 'Sanhedrin'". "An Interpreting Dictionary of Scripture Proper Names", New York, N.Y., 1869.

"In the writings of ancient Israel, most of the people listed are state officials of some sort-scribes, priests, kings and other bureaucrats. The emergence of writing closely followed the rise of early city-state structures, possibly as early as the Davidic-Solomonic period. [3] With the establishment of the monarchy, royal scribes were an essential component of a king's administration. Scribes kept written records of payments, royal correspondence and accounts of certain temple liturgies. [4] Furthermore, the scribal tradition used written reproductions of earlier traditions to not only teach the student to read, but to educate the scribe in memorizing aspects of their cultural tradition and develop their ability to recite and perform it. Thus, texts were critical in transferring key cultural traditions from one scribal generation to the next generation of scribal administrators and state elites."[19]

Quickly, let's pull out some facts about these priests, elders and scribes from **Numbers 11:14-17** that help solidify our scribal foundation:

- They were an answer to Moses's prayer.
- They were elders (already pastoring, guiding and leading the people)
- They were officers (priests, scribes, elders)
- They were handpicked by Moses.
- **They were called to lift the burden OFF Moses concerning the people.**
- There were called to work in unity amid the congregation.
- They were already working with the people as known leaders.
- They were known to be righteous, holy men by Moses.
- They were brought to the Tabernacle to stand before God and the people.
- They were called into *covenant* with Moses and with God.
- They were positioned to work with Moses at his leading and command.
- They were submitted to Moses.
- **They were ordained by God in the first corporate ordination in scripture.**
- **God came down from His throne to meet them.**
- **God ordained them DIRECTLY, personally.** No other group in the history of the Bible received this type of visitation or outpouring.
- **Scribes were ordained equally with priests and elders.**
- God *deliberately filled them* with Holy Spirit during a time when Holy Spirit only came upon people, but did not always fill them.
- They prophesied **(v. 26)**. In that moment, they were activated in prophetic ministry to serve with Moses.
- They were appointed to help judge the children of Israel.
- They formed the first administrative and instructional government set over the nation.

---

[19] Cameron Freeman, Scribes, "Prophets & Temple Priests: The process of establishing and maintaining Judean boundaries through the canonization of scripture," Socio-cultural Anthropology, http://cameronfreeman.com/socio-cultural/anthropology-religion-christian-tradition/process-establishing-maintaining-judean-boundaries-canonization-scripture/

According to Walter A. Elwell and Philip Wesley Comfort, Moses's council was set up like a tribal system.[20] These elders were already *heads of households* in their respective clans.[21] They note that these elders were instructed in the Law of Moses, and were given the authority to interpret the law, teach it to the people and administrate justice.[22] We learn that they were in charge of the preservation of the laws and often held court at the gates of each town.[23] **Ruth 4:1-12** notes what this specific aspect of the council entailed.

The council was known as the Great Sanhedrin **(Mark 15:1)**. The members of the council were the only ones in the kingdom who could try a king in court; expand the boundaries of the Temple and Jerusalem; answer questions and settle decisions concerning the Law. Cameron Freeman suggests that by the time the Second Temple period end, scribes had basically changed the Hebrew world!

He states, "By the end of the of Second Temple period, the vast number of scrolls referencing the authority of Torah on civil and criminal laws, stories and rituals had been firmly established and its application had grown in scope as various sects, such as the Sadducees, Pharisees, and Essenes expanded religious and cultural boundaries of the community."[24] I know this is an overwhelming amount of information. But I know that if you have made it this far, you are taking it in. There is a very critical point that I need to make here before moving forward.

First, we need to see that God was intentional in putting this group in a place of governmental authority. **Secondly, these 70 were installed into positions or offices.** They didn't just receive a gift. Third, they were intentionally divided into three groups: chief priests, elders and scribes **(Mark 15:1)** which indicates that each group had distinct functions; and that there were distinct roles among them. **Finally, we need to focus in on our specific group – the category of scribes and clearly see that they had been placed in "the office of the scribe" at this point.**

This changes everything for us as it relates to understanding scribal ministry. It reveals that (1) some scribes walk in the OFFICE of the scribe; (2) some people may have a scribal anointing upon them but not be designated to walk in a scribal office; and (3) that scribes were strategically positioned by God to have oversight – at some capacity – within all aspects of Kingdom affairs, especially at the elite or executive decision making level. Scribes were literally positioned over cities.

---

[20]Walter A. Elwell and Philip Wesley Comfort, "Tyndale Bible Dictionary: Elder," (Tyndale House Publishers: 2008), 414-415.

[21] Ibid, 415.

[22]Ibid.

[23]Ibid.

[24]Cameron Freeman, Scribes, "Prophets & Temple Priests: The process of establishing and maintaining Judean boundaries through the canonization of scripture," Socio-cultural Anthropology, http://cameronfreeman.com/socio-cultural/anthropology-religion-christian-tradition/process-establishing-maintaining-judean-boundaries-canonization-scripture/

The Reputation of the Scribe

For the most part scribes have garnered a negative reputation with the Body of Christ. Of all the things you hear about them, the majority are negative. The bad apples, so to speak, have been lumped with the good ones painting a picture that has been very difficult for some to purge from their minds – especially in our Western congregation. Today, they are best remembered for contending with biblical patriarchs, stirring up confusion and inciting the crucifixion of Christ **(Matthew 12:4; Matthew 23, Mark 3:22, Acts 4:5, 6:12).**

It is important to understand that not all scribes walked down this hell-driven, contentious path. In fact, the scribes Moses chose to serve with him on the original Sanhedrin were God-fearing scribes, lovers of the Word. Early scribes, particularly those in service to the temple, are believed to have been descendants of the tribe of Levi who had charge over temple serve[25] **(Exodus 32:29, Numbers 3:27-32, 4:4-15, 7:9; Lev. 8:17)**. In other words, their character and commitment to the Word was known.

One scholarly account summarizes the lineage of scribes this way:

> "In ancient Israel the scribal craft was principally confined to certain clans who doubtless preserved the trade as a family guild profession, passing the knowledge of this essential skill from father to son. Among the Kenites were "families of scribes" dwelling at Jabez (1 Chron 2:55). The connection between Moses' father-in-law, who was a priest (Exod 3:1), and the Kenites (Judg 1:16; 4:11) is an indicator that the art of writing was never far removed from the priesthood. During the united and later Judean monarchies a substantial number of scribes came from the Levites. The point of contact between the ritual and scribal functions derives from the demand for fiscal organization of temple operations (e.g., in Mesopotamia and Egypt most of the earliest writings are associated with temple records).

> "A Levite recorded the priestly assignments (1 Chron 24:6), and the royal scribe helped in counting the public funds collected for the repair of the Temple (2 Kings 12:10, 11; 2 Chron 14:11). Since the furnishing of written copies of the law was a (scribal) Levitical responsibility (Deut 17:18), the reforms of Jehoshaphat (cf. 2 Chron 17) cannot be disassociated from the scribal function. Although the extent of literacy within Israelite society is a complex question, at least one "writing prophet" found it convenient, if not necessary, to employ an amanuensis (Jer 36:26, 32), which strongly suggests that others did the same."[26]

Scribes, however, were ultimately scattered throughout Israel. By the time Christ's ministry begins, we hardly recognize their ancient roots... as they emerge in association with several religious sects of that time. Among the three most popular were: Pharisees, Sadducees and Essenes. There were others. We, however, are only going to address the two that were most connected to the scribes.

---

[25]Christine Schams, Jewish Scribes in the Second Temple, (England: Sheffield Academic Press, 1998), 87.

[26]Biblical Training, "Scribes, Scribes," https://www.biblicaltraining.org/library/scribe-scribes

As with all things, it only takes one bad apple to spoil the whole bunch. And such is the story of the scribes we meet at the brink of the New Covenant who were associated with the two most familiar political/religious sects in the Gospels: The Pharisees and Sadducees. Other sects included the Essenes, Herodians, and Zealots as well as independent groups like the independent high priests, elders, and scribes. During the time of Christ, politics and religion played a key role in the lives of the people.

> **FACT:** Not all scribes were Pharisees or Sadducees **(Matthew 15:1-3)**. Some were not a part of any political parties at that time other than their own order. Thus the popular phrase, "scribes AND Pharisees," which indicate two separate groups.

The Hebrew origin of the word Pharisee is *"parash"* and it means to separate, to make distinct, to declare, to pierce, to sting and to scatter. They were known as the "separated ones" and followed the Law of Moses in the strictest since. [27]
They observed the Sabbath, purity rituals, and believed in the resurrection, judgment, preserving the law, tithing, food restrictions, and the coming of the Messiah.[28] The thing is many of them – but not all -- refused to accept that Jesus was, in fact, the Messiah when He came. The Pharisees believed everything Torah taught…but some of them just didn't believe that Christ was standing right in front of them.

Take a look at **John 12:42** KJV: *"Nevertheless among the chief rulers also many believed on him; but because of the Pharisees they did not confess him, lest they should be put out of the synagogue…"*

Those who believed refused to confess Him. They would rather be liked by men, than favored by God. Does this sound familiar today? Sadly, those who rejected Christ (the compromising and the unbelieving ones) were also haughty, prideful, part of the ruling class, and enjoyed being the center of attention. Today, that would be equated to being "lovers of self" or narcissists.

Although this is not recorded in scripture, studies in the Babylonian Talmud show that there were seven types of Pharisee.[29] The first six were considered "plagues" of the Pharisees for false followers.[30] They were, in fact, actions or behaviors that some Pharisees exhibited to show how "holy" or important they were before the people.[31] It shows the depth and the length they would go to so that others could see them as being "committed" to their beliefs.

Seven Types of Pharisee

---

[27]The Works of Josephus, Book 18, (Peabody: Hendrickson Publishers) 2004, 477.
[28]Ibid.
[29]Mark Woods, "7 Familiar Types of Pharisee," *Christianity Today*, Jan. 19, 2016, http://www.christiantoday.com/article/7.familiar.types.of.pharisee/77087.htm
[30]Jewish Encyclopedia, The Hypocrisy of the Pharisee, http://www.jewishencyclopedia.com/articles/12087-pharisees
[31]Ibid.

(1) *The "Shoulder" Pharisee or Superficial Pharisee*: Named for wearing his good deeds on his shoulder so everyone could see them – on display. [32]

(2) *The "Wait a Little" Pharisee:* Named for finding an excuse for putting off a good deed or trying to wait to see how things work out before responding.[33]

(3) *The Blind & Bruised Pharisee:* Named for "literally" walking with their heads bowed or closed eyes to or avoiding looking at sin or anything unclean to remain pure. Because they weren't looking where they were going, they would bump into things and get bruised or injured.

(4) *The "Humpbacked" Pharisee:* Named for walking bent double, in false humility. This type, like the blind Pharisee mentioned above, wanted to make a public show of "humility" before others.[34]

(5) *The "Ever Reckoning" Pharisees*: Named for always counting up the number of his good deeds. This was a works-based "Pharisee."[35]

(6) *The "Fearful" Pharisee:* Named for always quaking in fear of the wrath of God, always fearful of punishment – which is the reverse of the kind of fear Father wants from us.[36]

(7) *The "God-loving" Pharisee:* Copied the life of Abraham who lived in faith and charity. This type of Pharisee was regarded well among others.[37]

These behaviors were so severe among the Pharisees that "R. Joshua B. Hananiah, at the beginning of the second century, calls eccentric Pharisees 'destroyers of the world' (Soṭah iii. 4); and the phrase "Pharisaic plagues"[38] became a common term. Further, it is noted that these are the types of scribes that confronted by Christ. Examine these seven descriptions closely; and read the woes in **Matthew 23**. Understanding the role of the Pharisees and Sadducees in biblical culture is significant for us today. Why? Well, because in the scriptures scribes were often mentioned in the same breath as these. The six negative characteristics shown above are indicators of some of the strongholds that we still face today.

Oddly, the Sadducees and Pharisees were opposing forces. They had strikingly different beliefs and were *constantly* at odds with one another - each group vying for a form of righteousness as well as greater influence and power among the Hebrew people than the other. The Greek origin of the word Sadducee, *saddoukaios*, is translated as "the righteous." They believed in the Law of

---

[32]Ibid.
[33]Ibid.
[34]Ibid.
[35]Ibid.
[36]Ibid.
[37]Ibid.
[38] Ibid.

Moses but did not believe it contained any revelation from God concerning Israel.[39] They did not believe in the resurrection, the immortality of the soul, the existence of spirits or angels, the end of the world or predestination by God.[40] They believed that the soul died with the body and that there was no afterlife.[41]

An entry in the Encyclopedia Britannica states: "The Sadducees were the party of high priests, aristocratic families, and merchants—the wealthier elements of the population. They came under the influence of Hellenism, tended to have good relations with the Roman rulers of Palestine, and generally represented the conservative view within Judaism. While their rivals, the Pharisees, claimed the authority of piety and learning, the Sadducees claimed that of birth and social and economic position. During the long period of the two parties' struggle—which lasted until the Romans' destruction of Jerusalem in 70 ad—**the Sadducees dominated the Temple and its priesthood**."[42]

In the world system, influence and power is known to determine the outcome of all things. Ironically, many believers think that Pharisees were ruling at the time of Christ. On the contrary, that was not the case. It was the Sadducees. At one point, the Sadducees filled nearly every seat on the Sanhedrin. In reviewing their belief system, you can see how this would be a problem! In addition, they had a reputation for using wealth to gain political and social affluence and power. Despite their differences, they were just as prideful and devious as the Pharisees. The difference here is that they were not "spiritually" invested in Christ's activities – the Pharisees were. Their disdain for him was more closely related to political impact verses Torah as I see it. So when it came to Jesus Christ, they joined forces with the Pharisees against him. The key here is this: Scribes were affiliated, in some capacity, with both groups. The most vocal members of these two sects had a hand in ruining the reputation of the scribe. Today, we hardly hear a single good word concerning them in traditional congregations in the Western world. Their reputations are synonymous with control, confusion, strife, bitterness, greed, selfishness, arrogance, pride and division. It's rare that we hear about their critical role in government or their indispensable contributions to our faith in antiquity or in present day.

In **Matthew 23:1-37,** Jesus made his thoughts about the *wayward* scribes and Pharisees very clear. He said, "*The scribes and the Pharisees sit in Moses' seat. Therefore, whatever they tell you to observe that observe and do, but do not do according to their works; for they say, and do not do. For they bind heavy burdens, hard to bear, and lay them on men's shoulders; but they themselves will not move them with one of their fingers. But all their works they do to be seen by men. They make their phylacteries broad and enlarge the borders of their garments. They love the best places at feasts, the best seats in the synagogues, greetings in the marketplaces, and to be called by men, 'Rabbi, Rabbi.'*"

---

[39]Encyclopedia Britannica, "Sadducee," http://www.britannica.com/topic/Sadducee
[40]The Works of Josephus, 477.
[41]Ibid.
[42]Ibid.

As we read through all of those passages, we see that Christ gave the scribes and Pharisees a strong rebuke. Let's break down what Jesus revealed concerning the condition of their hearts:[43]

- **They sit in Moses' seat.** They tried to establish themselves as the authority concerning the word of God. They tried to take the role of "shepherding and directing" God's people. Most importantly, this was an actual chair that they sought possession of as it was seen as a seat of authority before the people.[44]

- **Whatever the scribes and Pharisees tell you to observe, do it.** Jesus recognized that they knew the word of God and how to instruct the people to keep the word of God.

- **Do not follow their example.** Although they tell you to do the right things, Jesus said do not follow their example because they are not living the very lifestyle they profess.

- **They take pleasure in enforcing the law on others; but not on themselves.** Jesus is saying that scribes enjoy telling others what to do, and actually take pride in seeing people struggle to complete the hard tasks they place before them. Yet, they place themselves above the very things they demanded of others. They placed a higher value on themselves than they should have.

- **They do things so that men will see them.** Jesus said the scribes enjoyed drawing attention to themselves and being the center of attention. They performed certain acts for that singular purpose.

- **They make their phylacteries broad and enlarge the boarders of their garments.** Phylacteries are leather pouches that hold documents. In this case, the documents were perhaps copies of the law.[45] Here, Jesus is saying that they carried "large or big" leather pouches so that others could see them as they walked or prayed in public. Now consider this: These parchments were often *attached* to the forehead or to the arm. In addition, the Pharisees and scribes literally designed their clothes to *stand out* as holy or righteous garments before the people.

---

[43]Note: There's no doubt that the Scribes were diligent about preserving the written Word. They even went through painstaking methods of copying the Torah. Yet, they were intent on discovering hidden meanings not only in every word, but in every syllable and every letter of every word. Their investigation of the letter of the law was destructive of all spiritual instruction. Jesus clearly denounced peoples' dependence upon the "tradition of the elders" (Mark 7:7,8) and he pronounced "Woe to those "lawyers" who had taken away the key of knowledge, entering not in themselves, and hindering those who are trying to enter. When the Bible says that after Jesus had spoken they had been "astonished at His doctrine, for he taught them as one having authority, and not as their Scribes" (Matt. 7:28-29), there's no doubt about the contrast of Jesus teaching and that of the Scribes. Bible History Online, *The Authority of the Scribe*, http://www.bible-history.com/Scribes/THE_SCRIBESThe_Authority_of_the_Scribes.htm

[44]Note: SEAT, MOSES' (Μωυσε□ως καθε□δρας). The name given to a special chair of honor in the synagogue where the authoritative teacher of the law sat. The teacher in practice exercised the authority of Moses, in whom the written and the main lines of the oral law were regarded as originating. Not many of the Pharisees were actually scribes, among whose number there were also Sadducees. The scribes were looked upon as being the recognized exegetes of the law of Moses (Matt 23:2). E. L. Sukenik, Ancient Synagogues in Palestine and Greece (1934), 57-61; M. Avi-Yonah, Views of the Biblical World, Vol. V (1961), 63.

[45]Merriam-Webster's Dictionary Online, Entry: Phylactery, http://www.merriam-webster.com/dictionary/phylactery

- **They loved the best places at feasts, the best seats in the synagogues, and public greetings and recognition.** Jesus is saying that wherever the Pharisees and scribes went, they wanted to be recognized for their "authority or position" in society. It was so bad that they insisted on being greeted by titles in public places.

- **Christ called them hypocrites, vipers, brood of vipers and snakes.** The word hypocrite means "fraud or fake." A viper is a venomous snake with fangs that are hidden until the viper is threatened. When in attack mode, the fangs come out, penetrate its victim and inject poison into their system. Then, the viper follows its victim silently until it becomes paralyzed by the poison and dies. Only then, does the viper consume it. Snakes have varying descriptions in general, but what came to me here was the fact that the snakes first interaction with man was one based on deceptions, manipulation and control. Interestingly, the Jewish Encyclopedia also inserts the word "hyena" along with "viper" to present a stronger view of Christ's admonishment.[46]

- **Christ called them whitewashed tombs.** He described them as people who invest extensively in looking good on the outside, and looking like they are righteous and holy; but invest nothing on cleaning up their souls. He described them as filthy, selfish, lawless, self-indulgent people because their hearts were rotten.[47] He described them as being full of "dead-men's" bones.

- **They loved material goods and status.** Their dispositions were so negative that they had contempt for the very people over which they had rule and authority.

- **Christ condemned their behavior.** He reminded them that they were murderers walking in the way of their rebellious fathers. He stated that they had already condemned themselves and destruction would be their portion.

Perhaps the greatest part of this message, at least for me, is what Christ says next in **verses 34-36:** *"Therefore, indeed, I **SEND YOU** prophets, wise men, and **SCRIBES**: some of them you will kill and crucify, and some of them you will scourge in your synagogues and persecute from city to city, that on you may come all the righteous blood shed on the earth,* from the blood of righteous Abel to the blood of Zechariah, son of Berechiah, whom you murdered between the temple and the altar. Assuredly, I say to you, all these things will come upon this generation."*

It blesses me to know that Christ recognized that there were RIGHTEOUS scribes in His midst – those willing to die for His names sake. He said he would PERSONALLY send them! He said they would be killed and crucified, and scourged right in the center of their SYNAGOGUES and chased from city to city.

---

[46]Note: Jewish Encyclopedia, The Charge of Hypocrisy, it is such types of Pharisees that Jesus had in view when hurling his scathing words of condemnation against the Pharisees, whom he denounced as "hypocrites," calling them "offspring of vipers" ("hyenas"; see Ẓebu'im); "whited sepulchers which outwardly appear beautiful, but inwardly are full of dead men's bones"; "blind guides," "which strain out the gnat and swallow the camel" (Matt. vi. 2-5, 16; xii. 34; xv. 14; xxiii. 24, 27, Greek).

[47]Note: The white washed tombs of the Bible were actual "tombs" known as led sepulchers. First mentioned as purchased by Abraham for Sarah from Ephron the Hittite (Genesis 23:20). This was the "cave of the field of Machpelah," where also Abraham and Rebekah and Jacob and Leah were buried (79:29-32). In Acts 7:16 it is said that Jacob was "laid in the sepulchre that Abraham bought for a sum of money of the sons of Emmor the father of Sychem." It has been proposed, as a mode of reconciling the apparent discrepancy between this verse and Genesis 23:20, to read Acts 7:16 thus: "And they [i.e., our fathers] were carried over into Sychem, and laid in the sepulchre that Abraham bought for a sum of money of the sons of Emmor [the son] of Sychem." In this way the purchase made by Abraham is not to be confounded with the purchase made by Jacob subsequently in the same district. Of this purchase by Abraham there is no direct record in the Old Testament. Easton Illustrated Bible Dictionary, Public Domain.

He even reminded them of the atrocities of the past... in which Abel suffered and Zechariah were murdered between the TEMPLE and the ALTAR. Christ guaranteed that these things would come to pass. Then, he leaves them with one final declaration in **verses 37-39**. For me, it proves that even in the midst of this... Christ desired them to see truth. It reads: *"O Jerusalem, Jerusalem, the one who kills the prophets and stones those who are sent to her! How often I wanted to gather your children together, as a hen gathers her chicks under her wings, but you were not willing! See! Your house is left to you desolate; for I say to you, you shall see Me no more till you say, "Blessed is He who comes in the name of the Lord!"*

I say to you: "BLESSED IS HE... who comes in the name of the Lord!"

I want to share one more example with you. In **Mark 12**, the Sadducees were mocking Jesus. They had been asking questions in an attempt to trick him. The Pharisees were standing nearby listening when Jesus finally confounded them with wisdom. After the Sadducees were quieted, they gathered together and proceeded to test Him. One man, who was a scribe, asked him: *"Which is the greatest commandment of all?"*

Jesus answered the question: *"The first of all the commandments is: 'Hear, O Israel, the LORD our God, the LORD is one. And you shall love the LORD your God with all your heart, with all your soul, with all your mind, and with all your strength.' This is the first commandment. And the second, like it, is this: 'You shall love your neighbor as yourself. There is no other commandment greater than these."*

Then, the scribe said: *"Well said, Teacher. You have spoken the truth, for there is one God, and there is no other but He. And to love Him with all the heart, with all the understanding, with all the soul, and with all the strength, and to love one's neighbor as oneself, is more than all the whole burnt offerings and sacrifices*

Then Jesus said to him: *"You are not far from the Kingdom of God."*

Here is a perfect example of Christ recognizing that ALL SCRIBES were not evil.[48] This specific scribe walked into a realm of understanding WHO Christ was... and Christ acknowledged that he was on the threshold of believing. He prophesied to him – in that moment - stating he was on the right path toward God. In all of Jesus' dealings with the scribes, Pharisees and Sadducees this is one of the few times that we hear our Lord say something affirming. The scriptures tell us that not a single scribe or Pharisee asked another question after that **(Matthew 12:28-34)**.

I believe examining and studying these woes are critically important to the 21st century prophetic scribe. It's not enough to read through this section and move on. I believe each one of the points are worthy of detailed study and investigation. Why? Well, we desperately need to recognize the signs of a Pharisaic heart... and repent... overcome, receive deliverance, healing. Father said to me a few years ago, "It is our time prophetic scribes! Truly the first will be last and the last will be first! I am reviving a righteous lineage, a chosen people."

---

[48]Jesus did not condemn all Scribes and in fact they were not all bad. Nicodemus and Gamaliel were scribes and Hillel also for that matter. The young ruler who came to Jesus asking questions was no doubt a Scribe and Jesus said to him, "Thou art not far from the kingdom of God," (Mark 12:32-34) and He referred to some of His followers who would go to proclaim His truth as "scribes" (Matt 23:34). For the most part, however, they were considered to be cursed and the spirit of their instructions and teaching, as seen by all the records of them in the Talmud, are the very antithesis of that of the gospel of Christ. Bible History Online, Jews & the Scribes, http://www.bible-history.com/Scribes/THE_SCRIBESJesus_and_the_Scribes.htm

Knowing our history is so critical! No longer can people sit back, steal our heritage and tell us who we are based on a Greek Educational System. We are MORE THAN WRITERS! Knowing the history of scribes in the bible – the good, the bad and the ugly, brings freedom, releases knowledge... gives us understanding. After walking this ministry out for nearly two-decades now, I can assure you that many present day, prophetic scribes are operating out of many of these strongholds – some unaware. A scribe who lacks humility and who fails to see their own condition is as dangerous today as in the times of Christ.

> **FACT:** The Apostle Paul was a Pharisee, so was his father from the tribe from the Tribe of Benjamin. He was also trained under the head of the Sanhedrin, Gamaliel. **(Acts 22:3, 23:5-6)**

The First Ministry of the Scribe

In the previous section "Scribes of Old," I mentioned that the first ministry of the scribe, particularly the temple scribe, was that of a teacher of the word. This understanding comes from my personal study in the scriptures, and realizing that the most important thing that the Hebrew people had was the Word of God, and the most important thing to God was seeing them stay rooted in the Word. Whatever contribution revealed concerning the scribe in **Numbers 11**, their leadership roles began and ended with the quest of this new found governmental body to follow the way of the Lord – literally and by example.

All of their preparation and training wasn't solely for service inside the temple walls through natural skill and talent. They also played significant roles in teaching and guiding the Lord's people by rightly dividing the word of truth – and LIVING the life before them. It was necessary – in the Old Covenant – for people to follow the letter of the Law. These teachers, often referred to as Torah Teachers and later Rabbis, were some of the most devout and committed men of the Bible, whose work and legacy are worthy of our respect and honor. In this day and time, you are more likely to find a prophetic scribe who has memorized multiple copies of his or her poetry or songs verses those who can quote scripture beyond the 23rd Psalm. How sad is that? Oh, if we knew our roots. Where would the scribe be without Torah? How would the people know how to serve God without Torah? It was necessary that they be taught, and this was the number one function of those scribes who would be raised up by Ezra... through yet another transition period in antiquity.[49] In fact, their number one priority was re-educating the people concerning their God. Remember, the people had been scattered and were coming back together for the first time. A great deal of their heritage, customs and understanding of the Word had been lost across generations. You see, we are in this situation today! It's no wonder that God has raised us up for such a time at this. This particular entry can be found in the Jewish Encyclopedia:

---

[49]Isidore Singer, M. Seligsohn, Wilhelm Bacher, Judah David Eisenstein, *The Jewish Encyclopedia*, Scribes, http://www.jewishencyclopedia.com/articles/13356-scribes

The main objective of the scribe was "to teach the Torah to the Jewish youth in particular. It was they who established schools, and they were particularly enjoined to increase the number of their pupils (Ab. i. 1). Their mode of teaching is indicated in Neh. viii. 8: "So they read in the book in the law of God distinctly, and gave the sense, and caused them to understand the reading." This passage is explained by the Rabbis as meaning that they first read the Hebrew text and then translated it into the vernacular, elucidating it still further by dividing it into passages…"[50]

These scribes were IMMERSED in God's Word. They were not casual learners. In order to teach and impart at this level, they sacrificed their entire lives. This kind of loyalty, commitment and dedication is rare among the body today. Can you imagine what life would be like if we loved God and His Word from a place of saturation? Yes, there were some wayward scribes – but I tell you, there were also many faithful scribes in scripture.

What better way to destroy a legacy – especially one that was to be inherited with the engrafting of all men – than to bury the truth beneath another educational system. Yes, the Greek system of education is what we are accustomed to today, not the system of learning that God put in place in **Deuteronomy 6**. The standard of a teacher matters. In fact, I want you to consider scribes as educators! I love this description much more than simply saying teacher. Why? Because anyone can teach. These specific scribes *dedicated their lives* to making sure their students received understanding concerning whatever subject they taught. Remember, anyone can teach but not everyone is dedicated to the educational process of others.

So even as we use the term "teacher" from this point forward, I want you to set it in your heart that **we are talking about a guild or company of "educators"** who were committed to teaching God's Word as He released it to the Hebrew people. Keep in mind that their level of maturity, by the time they were released was epic… by our standards. Their lives, knowledge of the Word, knowledge of the will of God… and skill was exemplary. We need our foundation in Jesus Christ – not in this world. The first mantle of the scribe is this: Teach God's Word, not the way of men.

Scribes, Protectors of the Word

Matthew 5:17-19: *Think not that I am come to destroy the law, or the prophets: I am not come to destroy, but to fulfill.* ***For verily I say unto you, till heaven and earth pass,*** <u>***one jot or one tittle shall in no wise pass from the law, till all be fulfilled.***</u>

In addition to being interpreters and teachers of the Word, Jewish texts point out that scribes were also "protectors" of it. The Hebrew root of the word protect is CATHAR and it means:

- To hide, conceal
- To be hidden, be concealed
- To hide carefully

---

[50]Ibid.

- To be hidden carefully
- To hide oneself carefully

Remember, the Torah, also called the Sefer Torah, is considered to be the *exact* words of God as given to Moses. The trouble with this term, at least for the New Covenant believer, is that in Jewish understanding of it also refers to the complete written Torah (the five books of Moses) as well as Oral Torah - Mishnah, Talmud; and perhaps other relating writings. I must note, however, that it is believed that "oral law" is also the direct words of God to the Jews for maintaining the scriptures.[51] It is often referred to as placing a "fence around the law."[52] This statement brings greater clarity to our discussion here:

> "It was even believed that the oral law had been given by God Himself along with the written law to Moses on Mount Sinai. It was taught that the written law cannot be understood without the oral, and therefore the oral law was more important just like water and wine, both are important but one is much more valuable in the marketplace. By building a "hedge about the law" or fence around the law, the Jewish leaders would be able to develop a system of rules and interpretations that would keep people as far from sin as possible. For example, if the law said not to work on the Sabbath day, they would make up volumes of rules that indicated exactly what actions constituted work. This made a huge separation between the so-called righteous and the sinners.

> "It also made following God a burden that Jesus Himself said was too heavy to carry. It also allowed the leaders appear to be righteous, to approve and disapprove of people and to control all of the religious affairs within Judaism."[53]

For the majority of Protestants, our faith is rooted in the canonized Old & New Covenants – period… sixty-six books and no more. What is critical for us to see here, however, is the extent that scribes of old went to preserve and protect God's written Word. These oral laws are still in practice in Judaism today. The significance of this is simple: How are we, as present day scribes, expected to preserve and protect the Word of God today? Are we still mandated to uphold the integrity and character of the word – not only in our writing, but in our lives? What does this look like? Who is our greatest example? These are the questions we must ask – especially those who have embraced what it means to write prophetically. (We will discuss that in great detail later.) While we are not sofer scribes, we do have a responsibility to uphold God's intent and purposes – *uncompromisingly*. In seminary, we are taught that the "scripture cannot mean anything other than what the author intended." I firmly believe this. It is clear, through the painstaking work of sofer scribes… that they have managed to preserve the Old Covenant with an amazing level of accuracy over the centuries.

---

[51]Bible History Online, Fence Around the Law, http://www.bible-history.com/Scribes/THE_SCRIBESA_Fence_Around_the_Law.htm
[52]Ibid.
[53]Ibid.

And let's not forget about the preservation of the prophets and wisdom books. Somehow, through all the wars and challenges faced – these texts were fiercely protected – hidden, concealed. Once, I heard the Lord to say to me: "I hid them as surely as I hid my plan to bring forth my son to redeem the world."

By no means are we to follow the letter of the Law as they did, but we can glean a great deal about what it means to be loyal and committed to God as a son. In addition, I will share some of the requirements of a sofer scribe below. While we are not sofer scribes, the prophetic scribe IS in service to the King. Our heart condition, loyalty and dedication to God personally as well as our calling should STILL REFLECT on our ancient roots. We have a rich… apostolic and prophetic heritage through them!

We can't simply ignore the patterns, types and shadows revealed. With that understanding, let's take a look at what was required of them when writing a "Sefer Torah," the five books of Moses:[54]

- A Sefer Torah must be written by a Sofer (a specially trained scribe).[55]

- All materials used for the Sefer Torah must be Kosher, satisfying the rules of Jewish Law.[56]

- **The scribe must learn 4000 laws of Safrut must know before he starts writing the Sefer Torah.[57]**

- There are 304,805 letters in a Sefer Torah. If only one letter is missing the whole Torah is Pasul (not Kosher). If there is an extra letter it is also Pasul. Substituting one letter with another is also NO good. 99 percent Kosher = 100 percent Pasul (not Kosher).[58]

- There are 248 pages in a Sefer Torah.[59]

- Each page has exactly 42 lines.[60]

- **Even the spacing between words & paragraphs must be exact.[61]**

- The Torah must be hand written on Parchment [animal skin].[62]

- The parchment must be made from a Kosher animal.[63]

- **The ink, all ingredients used to make it must be Kosher or synthetic.[64]**

---

[54]Torah Tots, "What is a Sefer Torah," http://www.torahtots.com/torah/sefertorah.htm
[55]Ibid.
[56]Ibid.
[57] Ibid.
[58]Ibid.
[59]Ibid.
[60]Ibid.
[61]Ibid.
[62]Ibid.
[63]Ibid.
[64]Ibid.

- The ink must be black (not dark blue or any other color).[65]

- The giddin (thread) used to sew the parchments together must be made from the veins of a (Kosher) animal, and is specially treated for this purpose.

- The quill [the pen] must be from a Kosher bird - usually a goose or turkey.[66]

- The Sofer (scribe) must be Bar Mitzvah, 13 years old [some say even married].[67]

  o Must be fluent and tested in all the laws of Safrut - (laws of writing the Torah).[68]

  o Must be a certified Sofer.[69]

  o Must write with his right hand or left if he is a lefty.[70]

  o Must have the proper intention, when writing the Torah and especially when writing G-d's name.[71]

  o There is a special writing style with "crowns" (crows-foot-like marks coming up from the upper points) on many of the letters that they must learn. This style of writing is known as STA"M (an abbreviation for "Sifrei Torah, Tefillin and Mezuzot," which is where you will see that style of writing).[72]

Look at all of these requirements! Can you imagine this simply being a small fraction of what scribes of old had to learn and were required to implement? These are the ancient efforts that went into PROTECTING and PRESERVING God's Word. Today, this is still a part of our preservation process; but we also know that the best way to preserve God's Word is to live it! Without these diligent measures and more, you and I would not have the Old Covenant today. I also want to share this tidbit of information about the finished Torah. Check this out:

"The Torah is dressed and decorated because it is holy and is considered the core of Hashem's communication with Bnei Yisroel (The Children of Israel, i.e. The Jewish People). The tops of the wooden rollers of the Sefer Torah are often decorated either with rimonim or adorned with silver or gold crowns which covers both rollers, symbolizing G-d's sovereignty. It emphasizes the metaphor of the Keter (crown) of the Torah. The Torah is sometimes adorned with a breastplate, while richly decorated mantles cover and protect it."[73]

---

[65]Ibid.
[66]Ibid.
[67]Ibid.
[68]Ibid.
[69]Ibid.
[70]Ibid.
[71]Ibid.
[72]Ibid.
[73]Ibid.

Listen, we are still challenged with doing our part in protecting the Word of God today – both Old and New Covenants. For the prophetic scribe, there should be a burning desire to ensure this in the midst of every scribal project placed in our hands. The Apostle Paul said this in **2 Corinthians 3:2,** *"The only letter of recommendation we need is you yourselves. Your lives are a letter written in our hearts; everyone can read it and recognize our good work among you."*

We are 21st century protectors and preservationists of God's Word. Our hearts are set on ensuring that the weight, glory and meaning of the scriptures – as He originally released them to us, remains intact.

On the next page, note that I am sharing a chart of some of the Biblical scribes in the Bible. Take the time to review the scriptures, and examine the context in which they served kings. This may help you in gaining a better understanding of the scribal function in the scripture.

CHART OF SOME BIBLICAL SCRIBES

Scribe & Meaning of Name	Administration	Scripture References
Mithredath "Given by Mithra, Sun" Hebrew Meaning	King Cyrus	Ezra 1:8
Seraiah "Jehovah is Ruler" Hebrew meaning	Scribe to King David	2 Samuel 8:17 2 Kings 25:18, 23 1 Chronicles 4: 13, 14, 35 1 Chronicles 6:14 Ezra 2:2; Ezra 7:1 Nehemiah 12:1, 12
Sheva "Jehovah Contends" Hebrew meaning	Scribe to King David	2 Samuel 20:25
Shebna "Vigour" Hebrew meaning	Scribe to King Hezekiah	2 Kings 18:18, 37 2 Kings 19:2; Isaiah 36:3, 22 Isaiah 37:2
Joah "Jehovah is brother" Hebrew meaning	Scribe to King Hezekiah	2 Kings 18:18 2 Kings 18:37
Shaphan "To Cover or Hide" Hebrew Meaning	Scribe to King Josiah	2 Kings 22:3 – 14 2 Chronicles 34:8, 15-20 Jeremiah 36:10
Shavsha "Nobility" Hebrew meaning	Royal scribe to King David	1 Chronicles 18:16
Nethaneel "Given to God" Hebrew meaning	Scribe to King David	1 Chronicles 24:6 2 Chronicles 17:7 2 Chronicles 35:9
Jehonathan "Jehovah has given" Hebrew meaning	Scribe to King David	1 Chronicles 27:32 Jeremiah 37:15, 20 Jeremiah 38:26
Jeiel "God sweeps away" Hebrew meaning	Scribe of King Uzziah	2 Chronicles 26:11
Shimshai "Sunny" Aramaic meaning	Scribe of Rahum	Ezra 4:8,9 Ezra 4:17, 23

Scribe & Meaning of Name	Administration	Scripture References
Ezra "Help" Hebrew meaning	Scribe to King Artaxerxes of Persia	Ezra 7:6, 10, 11 Ezra 10 Nehemiah 8:1-3
Zadok "righteous" Hebrew meaning	Scribe appointed by Nehemiah	Nehemiah 13:13
Elishama "My God has heard" Hebrew meaning	Scribe to King Johoiakim	Jeremiah 36:12, 20, 21 Jeremiah 41:1
Baruch "Blessed" Hebrew meaning	Scribe to the prophet Jeremiah	Jeremiah 36:2, 27, 32
Elihoreph "God of Winter" Hebrew Meaning	Served in King Solomon's Court	1 Kings 4:3
Ahijah "Brother of Jehovah" Hebrew Meaning	Served in King Solomon's Court	1 Kings 4:3
Jehoshaphat (The son of Ahilud) "Jehovah has judged" Hebrew Meaning	Served in King Solomon's Court	1 Kings 4:32; Samuel 8:16, 2 Samuel 20:24
Jonathan the scribe "Jehovah has given" Hebrew Meaning	Served the Prophet Jeremiah	Jeremiah 37:15, 20
Tertius "Third" Greek Meaning	Served the Apostle Paul	Romans 16:22
Zenas "Jupiter" Greek Meaning	Righteous scribe and friend of Paul	Titus 1:1, 3:13
Luke "Light-giving" Greek Meaning	Served the Apostle Paul	Luke 1:1-4
Gemariah "Jehovah has accomplished" Hebrew Meaning	Served in King Josiah's Court	Jeremiah 36:11-20
Gamaliel "Reward of God"	Mentor to Paul, High Ranking Scribe	Acts 5:33-35, Acts 22:3

Note: Names are of great significance in bible. What does your name mean?

PRESENT DAY SCRIBES

There are so many people walking around saying, "I'm a scribe." I think it is a common fad these days among believers to claim something because it sounds good or because they seem to exemplify a sign or two of a specific office or calling. The ministry of the scribe, however, has way more to do with the heart condition and loyalty of the scribe toward God in the midst of their calling than it does the ability to function in the gift. Honestly, many present day scribes do not have the discipline, training or skill it would have taken to walk in the same league as the priestly scribes of old. We must remember, that scribes of old made God their singular priority. It was never about building one's own empire, but building the Kingdom that supported the community of believers. We are *very different* from the scribes of old. This isn't negative. It just speaks to this truth: We walk under a new and better covenant through Christ. Now, however, it is time to look at and acknowledge those differences – not simply from a place of comparison, but from the perspective of learning who we are and what our gifting and calling looks like in the 21st century. We are moving forward with this declaration: **We ARE NOT scribes of old!** Nor is it our intent to become scribes of old or present ourselves as such.

I firmly believe that if we plan to understand the present, it is absolutely necessary that we know our past. Our identity is tied in our rich, powerful biblical history. Remember, genealogy is critically important to God. Were it not so, there would be no need to know the lineage of Christ or that of Moses and Abraham. History provides us with a root system – a firm planting in the ground from which to draw wisdom, to understand why we do what we do... and to have a strong foundation on which to advance and continue to build. Right now, scribes often draw from the "wrong" history as it relates to our identity! Can you imagine believing that you were from a specific family tree only to learn one day it was all a lie? That would mean that literally EVERYTHING you thought to be true about yourself was completely fabricated. Well, in many ways that is where we are as a congregation when it comes to literary ministry, the gift of administration, writing, publishing, etc. We have to choose to know the truth.

Our scribal history is significant because it is about GOD'S DESIGN for us, not the design of men and its institutions. Every believer OWES IT to themselves to learn about their deep, spiritual heritage. Deep really does call unto deep! There is nothing wrong with going deeper in the things of God and refusing to remain in the shallows of understanding. This area, however, will be fought fiercely by some because it destroys nearly everything they have believed and understood. I cannot begin to tell you the opposition this teaching has faced. But I will tell you this: it has been worth every single struggle! I have no regrets.

So, I want to remind you that even though we've covered a great deal of Old Covenant insight, we are not—and I repeat... NOT scribes of old. However, we are the spiritual *descendants* of the faithful few who walked with God in Spirit and in truth. Our conception and birth was a supernatural one that took place in the book of Acts on the Day of Pentecost when Holy Spirit was released upon *all men*. All men were given the opportunity to walk in a level of personal freedom that never existed at this level before. We were activated for whatever purpose God had designed for us through Christ Jesus.

As we move forward, keep in mind that we live in a climate that can barely be compared to the climate of Moses, David, Ezra, Christ or the apostles. Specifically, I am speaking of the level of commitment these great men and their followers carried for God. This is especially true for those of us who struggle against the relaxed, and culturally-relevant-Gospel that is preferred by many. Simple things we take for granted like reading, writing and education was considered a privilege and honor during those times. Scribes of antiquity did not have the privilege of hearing the voice of God at will. Remember, God primarily spoke to priests and prophets back then or specific people whom He chose. Holy Spirit had not fully come in the earth, and was only released for certain assignments.

Holy Spirit came upon certain men at God's command and imparted at God's command. And even then, only a select few people experienced this type of outpouring. This gives new meaning to the second part of **Luke 12:48** which reminds us that to whom much is given, much more will be required. One of the most significant aspects of the **Numbers 11** ordination and sending of the 70 was that THESE SCRIBES received an outpouring and visitation of Holy Spirit! They were given an encounter that released and activated them in their ability to be of sound help to Moses. But even then, God did not release too much power. He allowed them to activate the prophetic **(v.26)**, but afterward He shut it down so that they would remain in their proper place as leaders' subject to Moses' authority. Look at the wisdom of God in that!

Look at us? We are CONSTANT CARRIERS of Holy Spirit! We have way more access to the Spirit than they ever had. We have more than an outpouring or an activation. Holy Spirit literally DWELLS in us. What does this mean? It means that much more is REQUIRED of us because of the expanse and extent of the untold riches that we have! The scribes of old could not freely NAVIGATE the supernatural realm the way WE are released to in this dispensation of the Gospel. Oh how blessed we are! How thankful we are for Christ's sacrifice. **It also gives us a unique view of just how devoted these scribes of old must have been to have sacrificed their lives based on "sheer will" and the desire to "please God" with such limited access to His Spirit.** To attempt to claim the heritage these godly men revealed to us through the scriptures would be presumptuous since the level of respect they garnered for righteous living has not been achieved by many to this very day – even with the FILLING of Holy Spirit! These godly scribes paid a high price for their calling, skill and legacy. I pray that this brief teaching, up to this point, has challenged us to honor their legacy – not curse it based on the actions of a few.

In this moment, we must SEE that our "scribal ministry" began when Holy Spirit unleashed the Spirit of Prophecy. We walk under the "present day" anointing of the scribe – not an Old Covenant anointing. There is a fresh revelation that God desires to release that will establish us in the present concerning our vocation. Take a look at this passage:

Acts 2:1-4, 17-21 says, *"When the Day of Pentecost had fully come, they were all with one accord in one place. And suddenly there came a sound from heaven, as of a rushing mighty wind, and it filled the whole house where they were sitting. Then there appeared to them divided tongues, as of fire, and one sat upon each of them. **And they were all filled with the Holy Spirit** and began to speak with other tongues, as the Spirit gave them utterance...*

But this is what was spoken by the prophet Joel: And it shall come to pass in the last days, says God,

*That I will **pour out of My Spirit** <u>on all flesh</u>;*
***Your sons and your daughters shall prophesy**,*
Your young men shall see visions,
Your old men shall dream dreams.
And on My menservants and on My maidservants
I will pour out My Spirit in those days;
And they shall prophesy.
I will show wonders in heaven above
And signs in the earth beneath:
Blood and fire and vapor of smoke.
The sun shall be turned into darkness,
And the moon into blood,
Before the coming of the great and awesome day of the LORD.
And it shall come to pass
That whoever calls on the name of the LORD
Shall be saved.

We were given life here... in this place. This outpouring is one of the greatest benefits of Christ's life, crucifixion, death, burial and resurrection in heavenly history. Now, *all born-again* believers – meaning those who believe on Jesus Christ and have been regenerated by the power of Holy Spirit - have the God-deposited ability to hear the voice of the Lord, navigate their lives by His Spirit and --- *prophesy*. Does this mean that every believer will prophesy? No. Many deny the operation of this prophetic gift in their lives and/or have yet to tap into it. When we are open to these unique experiences, I really believe Holy Spirit steps in to demonstrate God's power in this area.

If you are skeptical, I challenge you to trust Holy Spirit right now! Ask Him to release you in that gift of discernment and the gift of prophecy. If your heart is sincere, He will do it... and no man will have need to convince you. This I know.

Every believer has the potential to prophesy – to hear from Father and interpret His will and purpose! Yet, not every believer will allow Holy Spirit this kind of access in their lives. In light of this, a PROPHETIC SCRIBE is only PROPHETIC if they are operating out of the supernatural power that Holy Spirit alone is able to release whether they are aware of the prophetic or not. I have met many believers who write (or administrate other scribal offices) from a place skill and intellect alone – there is no conscious understanding of being personally inspired or prophetically motivated. The anointing is upon many of them. Yet, I cannot imagine how much further they could go in the Spirit if they knew who they were and operated intentionally in the midst of their ministry. The scripture below says it best.

1 Corinthians 14:39 AMP says: *"So [to conclude], my brethren, **earnestly DESIRE and SET YOUR HEARTS** on prophesying (on being inspired to preach and teach <u>and to interpret God's will and purpose</u>)..."*

We have complete access to HIS WILL & PURPOSE! Every time I think about this I am overwhelmed. There is so much we can learn from **1 Corinthians 14:39!** Clearly, our Father wants speak to us and through us. He wants us to know how to preach, teach and interpret his will and purpose for our lives and for His Body. He wants to give us great revelation and understanding concerning His Word. He desires to uncover the mysteries hidden in the scriptures since the beginning. We may not be scribes of old; but by the power of the Living God we can set our sights on a higher calling and perfect the excellence in our ministries and ministrations of the gifts within us.

We are *present day scribes* destined to write, record, demonstrate and interpret the heart and mind of God at His direction! Take a look at the chart on the next page, **The Emergence of Scribal Ministry.** It highlights *some* of the most distinguished roles scribes played in antiquity; and parallels these roles with the ministry of scribes today.

The Emergence of Scribal Ministry

Summarized Roles of Scribes of Old	Roles of 21st Century Scribes
Clerk: Recorded laws and decrees and read them in public; Taught others to read, interpret and understand the law; Recorded genealogy; Counted money and kept financial records	Accountant Money Changer Publican Genealogist Bookkeeper/Treasurer Speaker/Orator Librarian/Archivist/Historian Teacher, Educator
Secretary: A person entrusted with the correspondence and affairs of an administrative office	Secretary, Receptionist, Transcriptionist
Recorder: Drafted documents under the king's guidance; Prepared drafts of the royal will for the scribes; Recorded and reported events (including dreams, visions), activities; Drafted deeds and managed all treaties concerning the kingdom; Guarded the national archives and records; Conveyed heavy matters of kingdom concern to the king.	Writer (Devotions, Instruction, Novels, etc.) Journalist (Print, Broadcast Media, Digital) News Reporter Courier Researcher Stenographer Court Reporter Court Artist
Advocate/Attorney: Defended those on trial or those who had been accused; A comforter	Attorney/Lawyer Mediator, negotiator
Judge: Power to make judgments or decisions concerning issues of law within the kingdom	Judge Arbitrator Moderator
Copyist: Made perfect hand-written copies of documents including copying the Law of Moses and the Prophets without error	Editor/Copywriter Transcriptionist Publisher/Printer
Officer or Chief Ruler: Heads of tribes, clans; High ranking scribal officials serving in kings court or kings military	Officer Commander Executive Officers
***This chart is not to be considered a complete list.**	

Three Levels of Prophetic Writing & Scribal Ministry

Now that we have given a pretty thorough view of the ministry of the prophetic scribe, we are going to begin the process of focusing more on prophetic writing from this point forward. There are more than 230 passages of scripture that relate to scribal ministry in the Holy Bible. They show scribes completing a specific task, describing a scribal task taking place or in some way reveal the ministry of the scribe in operation. In studying these passages, I soon realized that the ministry of the scribe reveals itself in three primary areas: (1) administration; (2) instruction, and (3) creativity.

In other words, all scribes will operate within their ministries out of an administrative, instructional or creative mind – which may or may not include writing or recording. For example, a scribe who is naturally gifted in writing or developing administrative documents might also be an excellent "administrator" of people or a gifted manager over people or projects. A scribe who specializes in writing or developing curriculums in the area of instruction may also be an excellent educator and teacher. A scribe who writes creatively through plays, skits, poetry, etc. may also be extremely creative in other areas outside of the writing arena like event planning, promotions or marketing. In some very rare instances, I have met scribes who walk at master levels in all three areas at the same time! Many people who are multi-talented like this are being groomed by Holy Spirit to equip masters, lead as a chief officer over God's people in some area or to provide multi-level apostolic support to other leaders. It is from this perspective that I use the term master scribe. We will, however, discuss this more later. Again, in our scribe schools, classes and workshops we go through this in much more detail. Father has also given me great prophetic insight and understanding into what this looks like from the developmental stages through high levels of mastery. Briefly, however, I want to review each level with you in its most basic sense. As you read the brief descriptions, I pray you see yourself more clearly.

> **The Administrative Level:** In general, administrative scribes are gifted to develop, write, implement and or manage administrative documents and affairs that include but are not limited to business letters, polices, procedures, contracts, grants, historical documentation, record keeping, employee manuals, business plans, finance, etc. They seem to have natural insight and understanding into the administration (including management) of all types of business matters in their areas of specialty. One of the keys here is that this insight comes naturally or effortlessly for them; and Holy Spirit is constantly and consistently providing supernatural ideas and support.

> Master scribes **will have** a passion to administrate people, resources and organizations. There will be an unmatched intolerance for disorganization and chaos. Many times, pin-point solutions will come to them supernaturally for the specific projects they are anointed and appointed to oversee. They are often self-taught, self-starters who, with additional training in their specific area, will become experts in their field of study. It is not unusual for scribes in this area to move completely out of the writing arena into oversight and executive or pioneering administration.

The Instructional Level: In general, instructional scribes are gifted in breaking down the word of God as well as concepts, ideas, etc. for the purpose of bringing clarity and understanding to others. They are gifted in instructing others on multiple levels – from that of a child to that of an educated adult. In some instances, they are assigned to a specific educational level so-to-speak. They have a hatred for ignorance and a passion to educate. Scribes anointed in this area may write and/or develop curriculums, books of instruction, workbooks, collections of prophecy, prayers, sermons, instruction from dreams or visions and/or other resources that increase knowledge, wisdom, understanding and proficiency in their area of specialty. Their writing and/or projects will always be strategically designed to meet *specific* needs within the Body of Christ.

Master scribes **will have** a passion to not only teach or educate, but to raise up educators. Once they reach this level, there will be concerted efforts to duplicate themselves. Master scribes are not only anointed to develop or write instruction; but to teach it fully and with authority, influence and power. They have a desire to see God's people get understanding in whatever area of specialty they are in. While they are not always self-taught, they have an uncanny ability to pick up concepts, learn them, tailor them to their needs and then apply those concepts to the learning process. This group will also be life-long learners, and have a tendency to constantly enroll in classes or workshops trying to learn new things.

The Creative Level: The creative scribe will generally start out with a serious passion for doodling, journaling and/or writing in a specific creative form – journalism, poetry, spoken word, skits, scripts, novels, calligraphy, penmanship, photojournalism, comic book writing and development, etc. Creative scribes are instinctively creative in multiple areas of their lives. They think off the grid… sometimes bordering the unusual. It is not unusual for a scribe in this area to bring writings or projects out of the dream realm or under the inspiration of God-directed visions verses what is obvious. Their heart, however, is NOT one of performance but one fully centered on ministry – regardless of where they may or may not be sent to release that creativity. For example, they may actually be in entertainment based arenas, but are not – at heart – entertainers themselves. In addition, their creativity is not limited to artisanry. They may also walk in the realm of radical, creative ideas as it relates to administration and instruction.

Master scribes who walk in this area long to see their work produce God-centered transformation in the hearts of others. Their creativity seeks to produce a deliberate outcome. Their passion for excellence might be seen as perfectionism, when in truth, they are working diligently by the Spirit to produce what they creativity see – for maximum natural and spiritual impact. It is not uncommon for those walking under this specific scribal calling to be misunderstood and under-valued at a greater level than the other two. They may also act as revolutionaries in their arena for always forcing or pushing the envelope way past religion and known structure. In addition, the ministry of exhortation and encouragement is the most commonly recognized and easily identifiable area of ministry in this area. Masters in this area will always long to raise up other masters without exception.

Finally, it is important to remind you again that some scribes will develop in all three of these areas over time. This area of development, however, is not skill alone – but maturity of character, knowledge and understanding of the present and perfect will of God. True masters will NEVER compromise Christ's will and purpose. They will never pull the people of God outside of His Word, will or intent. This is critical. People can master skill and talent with a Babylonian mindset. Even in this, others will learn from them. But those "called of God," put His intent first. We must have a right understanding of this… otherwise we will compromise and walk in confusion. The outward display of the gift alone – regardless of how pleasing it is to the eye or the level of skill that is displayed, is NOT the measure of a master scribe. It must rise right alongside a covenantal passion for Christ and His heart for reconciliation. Why? Because "master scribes" are those who rest in the hands of the Master.

The Purposes of Prophetic Writing

In addition to uncovering the three levels of prophetic writing and scribal ministry, there are also ten concise reasons why we are commanded to write. These reasons were also derived from those same 230 passages of scriptures previously mentioned. These reasons, along with a brief explanation of each one is listed below. I strongly encourage you to purchase *The Scribal Companion* student workbook as well. It provides a solid guide for walking you through this book, and especially this section. I pray that Holy Spirit will help you see your scribal calling unfold.

Purpose #1: The ministry of scribe was purposed to write a memorial unto God to be rehearsed and memorized for eternity.

> **Exodus 17:14-15**: *God said to Moses: Write this for a memorial in a book, and rehearse it in the ears of Joshua...* Other scriptures: **Isaiah 30:8; Jeremiah 36:2; Psalm 135:13; Deuteronomy 6:8-10, Matthew 26:13**

> *Biblical Examples:* Recounts of God's hand in the lives of Abraham, Isaac & Jacob; the history of Jesus' life and ministry; the story of the creation, etc.

> *Present Day Examples:* Recounts of the Brownsville Revival, Azusa Street Revival, miraculous testimonies of healings; Chronicling God's hand in the lives of men and women of God like Smith Wigglesworth, and others.

Purpose #2: The ministry of the scribe was purposed to record legally binding agreements and contracts between God and man, God and Jesus, and man and man.

> **Exodus 34:27**: *And the LORD said unto Moses, Write thou these words: for after the tenor of these words I have made a covenant with thee and with Israel.* Other Scriptures: **Exodus 34:26-28; Numbers 5:22-24; Esther 8:8; Acts 15:19-21**

> *Biblical Examples:* The first contract ever written was formed between God and man. The

greatest covenant ever recorded was between God and Jesus Christ. Other covenants were also made including marriage agreements, divorce decrees, treaties between countries, agreements between kings or military leaders, and multiple other types of legal agreements between men, etc.

Present Day Examples: Examples still include the documents mentioned.

Purpose #3: The ministry of the scribe was purposed to record genealogy or lineage

Psalm 87:5-7: *The LORD shall count, when he writeth up the people, that this man was born there.* Other Scriptures: **Genesis 5; I Chronicles 1; Psalm 87:5-7; Matthew 1.**

Biblical Examples: Bloodline and family history was significant to God. The generations leading up to the birth of Christ are recorded in detail in the scriptures. Other facets of lineage are also recorded, including those that strayed away from the Lord. The recording of history, occupations, priestly duties, etc. is still significant to the body today.

Present Day Examples: There are multiple studies of family history, cultures, religious affiliations and lineage on multiple levels that are available to us now.

Purpose #4: The ministry of the scribe was purposed to serve as a witness, evidence or proof of a thing relating to God or for a historical account.

Deuteronomy 31:19: *Now therefore write ye this song for you, and teach it the children of Israel: put it in their mouths, that this song may be a witness for me against the children of Israel.* Other Scriptures: **Judges 5; Chronicles 26:22; Ezra 5:10; Psalm 87:5-7; John 1:45; Jeremiah 36:2; Mark 10:4**

Bible Examples: Oracles of God were traditionally memorized in song so that the stories could be passed from generation to generation. The song of Prophetess Deborah and Barak, and the Torah are excellent examples. Other examples would be passages chronicling the lives of key patriarchs like Moses, Noah, Abraham, Isaac, Jacob, and the story of Jesus' life, crucifixion, death and resurrection.

Present Day Examples: Recording the evidence of biblical prophecies coming to pass; recording the goings-on in Israel and other key countries discussed in the scriptures; recording stories of idolatry and devastation; chronicling the miracles, signs and wonders that stand out as a witness to Jesus Christ; recording historical events, etc.

Purpose #5: The ministry of the scribe was purposed to inspire or encourage others in the things of God.

1 John 1:4: *And these things write we unto you, that your joy may be full.* Other Scriptures **Psalm 41:1; Proverbs 3:3; Ephesians 5:19; Revelations 3:7**

Biblical Examples: Some biblical examples might include the Psalms, Proverbs, the Song of Solomon, the story of Noah's salvation from the flood, etc.

Present Day Examples: Testimonies of triumph and victory; Stories of miracles, signs and wonders; songs, poetry, words of inspiration and hope; devotions, etc. Any creative writing that brings encouragement or edification.

Purpose #6: The ministry of the scribe was purposed to clarify instructions concerning vision, direction, order or plans revealed by God.

Habakkuk 2:2 says: *And the LORD answered me, and said, Write the vision, and make it plain upon tables, that he may run that readeth it.* **(Ezekiel 43:11)**

Biblical Examples: God released many visions and instructions to man, and required that they be recorded in some form of document or even in a book. He recorded the law, instructions for constructing Noah's Ark, the Ark of the Covenant, the Tabernacle, Daniel's Vision, the vision of John in Revelations, the instructions Jesus gave his disciples, and even specific instructions for priestly garments. The bible is full of instructions and plans that were recorded so that men might remember and follow them exactly as the Lord requested.

Present Day Examples: The Lord is still releasing detailed instructions that must be written through his prophetic people. These instructions are for individuals as well as the corporate body – just as they were back then.

Purpose #7: The ministry of the scribe was purposed to warn people of pending judgment.

1 Corinthians 4:14 says: *I write not these things to shame you, but as my beloved sons I warn you.* Other Scriptures: **Exodus 17:14, 15; 1 Corinthians 4:14; 1 Corinthians 14:37; 2 Corinthians 13:2; Colossians 3:16**

Biblical Examples: The Old and New Covenants are chock-full of prophetic warnings. Some of the most notable can be found in the prophets in the OT, and in the words of Jesus in the New Testament. There are also words of warning in many of the Psalms and Lamentations.

Present Day Examples: Many scripturally based prophetic words are being released in the form of letters, decrees and declarations, poems, songs, and other literary works.

Purpose #8: The ministry of the scribe was purposed to record the things you have seen, experienced and the things the Lord has shown you.

Revelations 1:19 says: *Write the things which thou hast seen, and the things which are, and the things which shall be hereafter...*

Biblical Examples: Some of the most notable examples are the visions the Lord showed Abraham concerning his seed. Other examples include the witness to Jesus Christ; the story of the church of Acts and the outpouring of the Holy Spirit; the vision the Lord showed John in the book of Revelations; etc.

Other examples include writings that exalt the Lord God, telling of his majesty and greatness.

Present Day Examples: Present day examples could include your personal testimonies and experiences with Jesus Christ; the recording of dreams and visions that the Lord has released to you, etc.

Purpose #9: The ministry of the scribe was purposed to record the things God reveals to your heart in a book.

Jeremiah 30:2 says: *Thus speaketh the LORD God of Israel, saying, Write thee all the words that I have spoken unto thee in a book.*

Biblical Examples: There are many examples in the scriptures of the Lord visiting certain men and women and speaking to their hearts. Many of these conversations are recorded in the scriptures. One of my favorite examples of this can be found in the story of Esther.

Present Day Examples: There are many things that the Lord reveals to us even now. This book is one example. Other examples are the many Holy Spirit inspired books that are emerging from men and women of God writing from inspiration.

Purpose #10: The ministry of the scribe was purposed to give an orderly account of things that happened, and to record the exact words of God.

Luke 1:3 says: *It seemed good to me also, having had perfect understanding of all things from the very first, to write unto thee in order...*

Biblical Examples: The exact words of God were recorded in the Ten Commandments, the laws governing priests, and other specific instructions given by God. In addition, Luke went back and researched the story of Jesus and put all of the events in a specific timeline that was accurate and easy to follow.

Present Day Examples: The recording of any activity, event or situation that is relevant to the things of God with complete accuracy and in a chronological manner.

SCRIBES INSTRUCTED

Christian writers are really biblical scribes – whether they are producing plays, movie scripts, writing poetry, novels; or publishing prophecy, health or wellness blogs or podcasts. Bringing believers into this place of understanding has been like breaking the glass ceiling for women over the past century. The Christian writing community FIGHTS this. Their roots are so entrenched into the Greek system of academia and the literary merit system, that it cannot see God's design clearly. This isn't a criticism; rather, it is a cry for an awakening. It is as if the spirit of the age is working overtime to keep this community entrenched in the academic tradition of darkness. Writing, and all other scribal activity associated with it, significantly impacts history. On a small scale, all we have to do is look at our history here in the United States and examine how certain books, movies, plays, etc. changed the way an entire generation thinks and lives.

Joshua J. Mark stated: "History is impossible without the written word as one would lack context in which to interpret physical evidence from the ancient past. Writing records the lives of a people and so is the first necessary step in the written history of a culture or civilization."[74]

For the Christian writing community overall, we are *still* at the beginning stages of returning to our writing roots… that of scribal ministry. The scribal anointing book series and the rise of prophetic scribes globally speak to this. I can still remember when the Lord released the prophecy in 2005 that the "The Scribal Anointing" was upon the land… and that it would take the Christian writing community by storm. That prophecy is continuing to unfold in the earth.

This is not a beat-up the Christian writer section. Rather, it is a cry for our community to see ourselves through the eyes of God's Word instead of through the world system, Babylon. It is true that writing has been recognized as being spirit-led by some, but the connection to the depth of scribal ministry is limited. Even if a believer does not embrace or accept the "prophetic" as you or I understand it… there is still great wisdom to garner from the long, historically proven journey of the scribe and every other gift and calling associated with its legacy. We cannot afford to ignore this.

In truth, a spirit-led writer is the same as prophetic writer in the sense that you seek to be directed by God in your writing initiatives. As believers, our core function is to magnify God in whatever we do. To ignore this is to ignore our call to represent Christ in the earth. As a community, we also need to see that the ministry of the scribe is a core, governmental function in the global congregation that touches absolutely every area of society. Our seeds and watering of writing has the power to change the world for Christ – one soul at a time! Unfortunately, prophetic writing is barely a fore thought. Because of a lack of understanding, ignorant ideals, fear of new revelation and the tendency to cling to old concepts and stay married to extensive misconceptions, it has been limited to a role walked out only in antiquity with no real relevance for today.

---

[74]John J. Mark, "Writing," *Ancient History Encyclopedia*, (West Sussex: April 2011).

We are changing this perception, these false beliefs. Scribes were God's original storytellers, poets, spoken word artists, orators, speech writers, etc. Scribes were the first, in collaboration with chief priests and elders, to build an administrative and instructional prototype from which we continue to build upon today. Scribes held the first writing classes and workshops for believers for goodness sake!

Despite what we may see, a remnant of believers are advancing. What is most visible (on television, radio, social networking sites, etc.) is an extremely poor depiction of what God is really doing in the midst of the congregation. Those activities, though real, can be distractions that - once deconstructed - provide insight into how the systems of this world seek to keep many believers bound in and by the Babylonian system. But guess what, there are fires ignited by God across this nation... and a remnant that is growing in power, remaining strong and standing true to their faith. As more of them learn about this aspect of their calling, they gain the tools needed to effectively administrate their scribal callings and offices.

Finally, I strongly believe our Heavenly Father is moving in ways that are "not so visible" among us. Small groups are having tremendous impact. We have seen the congregation advance through the spread of missions (to the United States), the defining and redefining of evangelism (in the 21st century), numerous pastoral ministry shifts (focus returning to team ministry, not the idol worship of one leader), the advancement of prophetic ministry overall and continued apostolic reformation. And as apostolic reformation continues, the ministry of the teacher has been revived, amplified... ensuring that the people of God can receive knowledge, understanding and wisdom – and walk in it. A great awakening is upon us, and I believe the understanding of "The Scribal Anointing" is the key to our revival. As we move into the heart of this book, I want to encourage you to determine in your heart, right now, to be a catalyst for our scribal reformation.

The Ezra Pattern

More than 32 scribes are mentioned by name in the Holy Scriptures. The most famous and notable scribe among them is the high priest, Ezra. His name literally means "Yahweh has helped"[75] or "help." [76] He is revered in antiquity and by theologians globally as the greatest scribe in ancient Israel. Based on the historical account in the book of **Ezra**, he single-handedly reorganized the order of the scribe for temple service – literally merging their past and present; and prophetically setting the stage for a national revival.

Upon returning to Jerusalem, the scripture reveals that:
- He brought the children of Israel back into alignment with God.
- He re-established unity among the people.
- He completely restructured Temple services.

---

[75]Orr, James, M.A., D.D. General Editor. "Entry for 'EZRA.'" "International Standard Bible Encyclopedia." 1915.
[76]Ibid.

- He created a completely new scribal order.
- He re-established the observance of Mosaic Law.
- He re-instituted covenantal marriage protocols forbidding intermarriage with heathen nations.
- He was a reformer.

Ezra apostolically led an exiled people out of Babylon and single handedly, with God's favor, back into the presence of God through his office as a priest and a scribe. Prophetically, this is a picture of the type of anointing we carry. Ezra was conscious of clearing out any and everything that pointed toward idolatry; and kept the people of God separated from Him.

Here is a strong summary of Ezra's contribution during the Old Covenant:

> "Ezra marked the watershed for the later development of the understanding of the scribe. Indeed, the transition is already suggested in the Book of Ezra: in the royal decree (7:12-26) "scribe" is used in an administrative sense, but in the narrative (7:6, 11) the term already refers to Ezra as a scribe who, by reason of his learning, is capable of interpreting the law for the common people. Moreover, by his priestly lineage (7:6) he symbolized the close connection between the priesthood and this official interpretation of the law which existed probably until the 2nd century BC. This connection appears to be the continuation of the association between scribal and cultic functions of an earlier day. By Pers. royal decree, the law of Moses was made civilly binding on Jews living 'Beyond the River' (i.e., W of the Euphrates, 7:25ff.). The essential task of interpreting Moses' law so that it could function in this new civil capacity was given to the priesthood (Ezra) and the Levites (cf. Neh. 8:6-9)."[77]

Now, let's take a quick look at Ezra's background. In doing so, you will see how all that we have covered up to this point can be seen demonstrated in the life of this famous historical figure.

According to **Ezra 7:1-7,** Ezra was the son of Seraiah a descendent of the house of Zadok which has its origins in the ancient Levitical priesthood. His lineage is thoroughly traced back to Aaron, the brother of Moses who was a chief priest among the Hebrew people. The scripture indicates that he came up from Babylon after the exile. Most scholars accredit him with authoring the 1 & 2 Chronicles, Ezra and Nehemiah. While it has not been proven, scholars and theologians have speculated that he may have authored Psalm 119. Ezra 7 also reveals that he was trained professionally as a scribe from his youth and was known throughout the land as a great orator, scholar, teacher and preacher of the Law. An interesting fact that many ministers of our day point out is that Ezra was the first priest in antiquity to speak from a podium before the people **(Nehemiah 8:4)**. Ezra's legacy begins in 459 BC when he leads the second body of exiles out of Babylonian to Jerusalem B.C. 459.[78]

---

[77]Ezra & the Intertestimental Period, BibleTraining.org, https://www.biblicaltraining.org/library/scribe-scribes
[78]M.G. Easton M.A., D.D., Illustrated Bible Dictionary, Third Edition, published by Thomas Nelson, 1897. Public Domain, copy freely.

He was gravely concerned about the religious state of the Jewish people, who had all but abandoned their faith and way of life during their exile. He had one mission: Unify the people of God according to the Law. It is noted that, "Ezra came at the head of a caravan of about 1,800 men, not including their women and children.

They made the four month journey from Babylon without the benefit of military escort, thereby demonstrating their trust and reliance upon God."[79] Ezra's impact was so significant that in **Nehemiah 8:7,** we see that he has raised up a team of "scribes" to assist him in making sure the people received understanding concerning the scriptures. Chris Keith noted the words of Josephus in reference to this saying that Ezra "appointed the Law to be the most excellent and necessary form of instruction, ordaining, not that it should be heard once for all or twice or on several occasions, but that every week men should desert their other occupations and assemble to listen to the Law and to obtain a thorough and accurate understanding of it."[80] I strongly encourage you to read the books of Ezra and Nehemiah – this time from a scribal perspective. I believe it will give you a deeper and broader understanding of why Ezra is so revered in antiquity.

In light of this history, let's take a close look at what is said about Ezra directly in the scriptures. I have not added my own spin on any of these facts. The scriptures, as you review them, literally state every single thing that is relevant to our discussion here. Hold these points in your memory, as they are at the very heart of uncovering The Scribal Anointing®. We learn that Ezra:

1. **Was a *skilled scribe* in the Law of Moses and *God gave the law* to him (Ezra 7:6).** This indicates that he went through training as a sofer scribe. It also indicates that the Lord placed a special anointing upon Him to understand and interpret the Law.

2. **The *hand of the Lord was upon him* and he walked in favor. (Ezra 7:6, 28)** This indicates that Ezra was sanctioned for his task, walked in God's blessings concerning his assignment and had access to everything needed to fulfill that assignment.

3. **Ezra *prepared his heart* to seek the Law of the Lord, to do it, and to teach it completely. (Ezra 7:10)** Ezra sought to make sure his heart was in alignment with God's will and purpose. He longed to fulfill both priestly and scribal office in spirit and truth.

4. **Ezra was described as a priest and a scribe in the Law of the God of Heaven. (Ezra 7:12, 7:21)** Ezra met the requirements of the Levitical priesthood and the requirements of a master scribe.

5. **Ezra blessed the Lord for giving him favor with the king and for granting him mercy. (Ezra 7:27-28)** Ezra heart was positioned in gratefulness, thanksgiving.

---

[79]Ezra Facts, Encyclopedia of World Biography. Copyright 2010 The Gale Group, Inc. All rights reserved.

[80]Chris Keith, Jesus Against the Scribal Elite, Baker Academic:2014, 33.

6. **Ezra fasted and prayed for humility (Ezra 8:21-23).** He recognized this stronghold in his life and sought to overcome it. He was thankful for all that God had done for him.

Ezra was the ideal picture of a Kingdom-centered scribe. **I have come to recognize these steps as the Ezra Pattern for scribes.** He had everything the scribes and Pharisees whom Jesus rebuked in **Matthew 23** lacked. His zeal for God superseded all else in his life – including his own personal safety and well-being. **He loved God and loved God's people**. He did not exist as a man on his own merit, but as a man fully submitted to the will and way of God.

Take a look at this in light of what we know about the preparation of a scribe. Consider the qualifications of priesthood in antiquity. Think about the hardship that he faced in exile while in Babylon. Can you imagine how difficult this was? Yet, we see him… taking on one of the greatest and most difficult tasks in biblical history. Our scribal pattern is Ezra, high priest and scribe.

Unveiling The Scribal Anointing

In **Matthew 13:10,** Jesus taught his disciples in multiple parables throughout the day. At one point, they approached him and asked, *"Why do you always speak to us in parables?"*

Jesus answered them and said: *"Because it has been given to you to know the mysteries of the Kingdom of Heaven, **but to them** it has not been given. For whoever has, to him more will be given, and he will have abundance; but whoever does not have, even what he has will be taken away from him. Therefore, I speak to them in parables, because seeing they do not see, and hearing they do not hear, nor do they understand."*

As strange as it may seem Jesus spoke in parables because He knew that those who believed in him would understand them. He knew that as relationship with Him grew, those parables would continue to unfold fresh revelation. Parables also ensured that those who did not believe that Christ was the Son of the Living God could never tap into the secrets and mysteries of the Kingdom. Jesus was protecting the Kingdom from scoffers and unbelievers. The parables were not intended to *confuse* the believer, but to confound and confuse those who rejected God. They were always meant to be revealed to those who belong to God.

As the day progressed, Jesus continued to teach them. When he was done, he asked them a very important question: *"Have you understood all these things?"*

The disciples replied, *"Yes, Lord."*

Then he said in **Matthew 13:52,** *"Therefore every scribe instructed concerning the Kingdom of Heaven is like a householder who brings out of his treasure things new and old."*

In all the parables that Jesus spoke that day this was the shortest. Father revealed to me that "in this moment" through these words all believers could teach and interpret God's Word. No longer would there be a need for an "elite class" of scribes such as those from the old regime. In one concise statement an ancient monopoly ended and a fresh anointing became accessible. **In other words, Christ was raising up scribes!**

Let's take a closer look at **Matthew 13:52**. The scripture has been retyped and keywords have been bolded and underlined – study them closely.

> "Therefore every **scribe** **instructed** concerning **the Kingdom of Heaven** is **like a householder** who **brings out of his treasure** things **new and old**."

In my study time, Holy Spirit led me to break down every aspect of this scripture through a thorough exegetical study. The end result was a greater understanding of what Christ was speaking to His disciples. Now take a look at this same scripture below. But this time, the bolded and underlined words above have been replaced with their Greek definitions to bring greater understanding. Please note that these are the exact words that corresponding words align with. Absolutely nothing has been added to change the meaning of the scripture. It reads:

> "Therefore every **writer, secretary or recorder** **who has become a disciple to follow [God's] precepts and instructions** concerning the **heart and mind of God** is like a **master of the house or owner** who **leads out or brings forth** of his **kingly, regal storehouse** things **uncommon, of a new kind or fresh** and **from an earlier time**.

Before moving forward, there are a few things I want to bring to your remembrance:

- The word *scribe* has multiple meanings. This means that any scribal function could be substituted here. It also means that if the scripture uses the term secretary, Torah Teacher, etc. that it is referring to the office of the scribe.

- The word *instructed* refers to being taught of the Lord or having been made a true disciple or student of the God.

- The reference to *"heart and mind of God"* speaks into knowing God's present will and purpose.

- The phrase *"master of the house"* can be traced back to the "elders and officers" from *Numbers 11*. The "master of the house" in biblical times were the chiefs set over specific clans or family household. While this isn't relevant in a literal sense, it speaks into the weight of spiritual maturity and leadership needed for present day scribes.

With this insight, I pray that your view of this parable is shifting. God is saying that every writer secretary or recorder who has purposed in his heart to follow Christ by living the word and obeying word is a master of his own house! This means that these scribes have made the right choices concerning their walk with the Lord and have denied the desires of the flesh. As a result the scribes will lead and bring forth wisdom, revelation, knowledge and understanding concerning the word of God that is uncommon and fresh, and from the times that have past.

This is The Scribal Anointing! For a more concise definition we can say this: It is the anointing that permeates the life of scribes who are "instructed" in the Kingdom of Heaven. It is walking out your ministry according to Father's original intent and purposes as revealed here. We are prophetic TREASURE HUNTERS who are revealing the heart and mind of God through our scribal calling! Please grasp this – we are not revealing OUR minds, but HIS mind! Now, let's take this understanding of **The Scribal Anointing®** to the next level. Let's look at what Christ was REALLY saying.

Remember, he declared that He speaks nothing except what he hears the Father speak; and repeats what He sees the Father do. This parable is an excellent example of that.

Ezra 7:6 says: "...and _he was_ a skilled (trained) scribe _in the Law of Moses, which the LORD God of Israel had given._"

Ezra 7:12 says, "...to Ezra _the priest, a scribe of the Law of the God of Heaven..._"

These passages mirror Christ's words in **Matthew 13:52**; but instead of saying "we must be like a scribe," they say that Ezra "was a scribe" instructed in the Law of Moses a scribe of the Law of the God of Heaven. **Clearly, Jesus was instructing us to pattern ourselves after Ezra the scribe's example.** Again, this wasn't a literal sense… but it was prophetic cry to examine the heart, mind and motives of Ezra's scribal ministry as a priest and a scribe.

The New Covenant, however, now supersedes the Law of Moses.

If you are still moving through this book right now, then you have probably been impacted greatly by this message and singled out as a present day scribe. Using Ezra's walk with the Lord as a roadmap, we can clearly see what God expects of us as scribes today… while clearly appreciating our scribal heritage. Together, we have uncovered an ancient treasure hidden in this parable Jesus spoke. Christ pointed us to Ezra's roadmap to becoming scribes instructed in the Kingdom of Heaven:

1. **We must be rooted in the word of God and able to recognize His voice.**

    Ezra knew how important it was to be able to hear and obey the voice of God. His scribal ministry exemplified **2 Timothy 2:15 AMP**, "_Study and be eager and do your utmost to present_ *yourself to God approved (tested by trial), a workman who has no cause to be ashamed, correctly analysing and accurately dividing [rightly handling and skillfully teaching] the Word of Truth."*

2. **We must prepare our hearts to receive divine instruction from God, to seek righteousness, to act upon his word and to teach it completely.**

Ezra revealed – through his life – what it means to prepare one's heart before God.

"For if anyone is a hearer of the word and not a doer, he is like a man observing his natural face in a mirror; for he observes himself, goes away, and immediately forgets what kind of man he was. But he who looks into the perfect law of liberty and continues in it, and is not a forgetful hearer but a doer of the work, this one will be blessed in what he does." -- James 1:23-25 Other relevant scriptures: **Deuteronomy 4:29-31; 1 Chronicles 28:9; Psalm 24:6; Psalms 32; Ephesians 6:17-18; 2 Timothy 4:1-5**

3. **We must remember that we have received gifts from God – not man - including the gift of administration; and God has made us kings and priests upon the earth.**

Ezra was a priest and scribe. He knew he could do nothing in and of himself without God. He was completely dependent on his Father in Heaven.

"And have made us kings and priests to our God; and we shall reign on the earth." – **Revelations 5:10** and **1 Corinthians 12:27-29**

4. **We should bless the Lord at all times and thank him for his grace and mercy at every opportunity.**

Ezra had something so many believers lack today – the fear of God and a heart overflowing with thanksgiving. As God blessed him and delivered him from the hands of the adversary, he immediately went into a mode of thanksgiving and worship. He never forgot how good God was to him or how worthy God was of his praise.

"Oh come let us sing to the LORD! Let us shout joyfully to the Rock of our salvation. Let us come before His presence with thanksgiving; Let us shout joyfully to Him with psalms. For the LORD is the great God, And the great King above all gods." -- **Psalm 95:1-3.** Also take a look at: **Ephesians 1:15-16; Psalm 100**

5. **We must fast and pray for humility.**

Ezra believed in living a chaste, holy life before the Lord. Fasting and praying were a part of that life, and he knew that a heart quick to repent could turn away the wrath of an angry God.

Ezra 8:21-23 says, *"Then I proclaimed a fast there, at the river Ahava,* **that we might humble ourselves before our God to seek from Him a straight and right way for us, our little ones, and all our possessions.** *For I was ashamed to request of the king a band of soldiers and horsemen to protect us against the enemy along the way, because we had told the king, The hand of our God is upon all them for good who seek Him, but His power and His wrath are against all those who forsake Him. So we fasted and besought our God for this, and He heard our entreaty."*

6. **Ezra knew that consistent obedience and faith gave him favor with God – kings recognized and yielded to his Kingdom authority.**

   Ezra 7:21-22 says: *"And I, even I, Artaxerxes the king, issue a decree to all the treasurers who are in the region beyond the River, that whatever Ezra the priest,* **the scribe of the Law of the God of heaven,** *may require of you, let it be done diligently,* **22** *up to one hundred talents of silver, one hundred kors of wheat, one hundred baths of wine, one hundred baths of oil, and salt without prescribed limit. Whatever is commanded by the God of heaven let it diligently be done for the house of the God of heaven. For why should there be wrath against the realm of the king and his sons?"*

When Christ declared **Matthew 13:52,** I am convinced that His disciples knew exactly what he meant. I am sure that their hearts went immediately to the legacy of Ezra – recounting his faithfulness before God. The EZRA PATTERN, in the spiritual sense, is critical to the ministry of the scribe today. When we grasp hold of this in our hearts our minds will change, our perceptions will change, our focus will change and our feet will be set on fulfilling the ministry inside us.

This is what Ezra did. And this, my brethren, is *The Scribal Anointing*. It is the God-given command, passion, gift and desire to write the rhema word of the Lord with biblical accuracy and soundness of doctrine from a sanctified heart; and to deliver those words to God's people no matter the cost.

> **FACT:** Ezra authored 1 and 2 Chronicles, Ezra, Nehemiah, and is believed to have written Psalm 119 – the longest psalm in the bible.

Implement the Ezra Pattern

The Ezra Pattern is the very foundation of The Scribal Anointing®.

I know that there are many scriptures you can pray, but I believe praying according to this pattern is extremely significant to your spiritual growth and development as a prophetic scribe. Soon after I received this revelation, I began to denounce the scribal strongholds outlined in **Matthew 23** that were and/or may have been effective in my life. In addition, I added anything else to this list as Holy Spirit revealed. I examined myself to ensure that my heart remained pure, open before God. Listen, we can never go wrong by posturing ourselves to rend our hearts at the feet of Christ.

I followed this act of faith with sincere repentance. Please note that I am not asking you to do anything long, drawn out or overtop. I know without a doubt that EVERY SCRIBE needs to do this, regardless of how free and mature we believe we are. The mere fact that someone would say, "I've done this already," or "God healed me of these things before" indicates that there just might be a level of self-righteousness and pride still lurking in the midst. At the end of the day, this truth remains: Doing it AGAIN will not harm you! Confession and repentance is a privilege and an honor.

In addition, I began confessing the six points from Ezra's Pattern over my life and scribal ministry. I can remember declaring, "I will bless the Lord at all times. I will walk in true humility. I am a scribe instructed in the Kingdom of Heaven." I declared and prayed until it became a part of my identity. I also declared and prayed these things over *every scribe* I have ever mentored and during every scribal event, encounter, etc. that the ministry has ever held.

I have prayed it over the ministries entrusted to me, those I oversee and guess what, I still use it as a foundation today… over a decade later. I always end my prayers with this decree (in some form): "*I am a scribe instructed in the Kingdom of Heaven, standing as the master of my house pulling out treasure things new and old and from ancient of days.*"

God's Word will never return to us void when we are postured to receive it. It has yielded much fruit and accelerated The Scribal Anointing® in me, and within the hearts of those who have caught the revelation here. When have we, as prophetic scribes and writers, ever had a Biblical prayer constructed for us… that ties in to the very heart of God? Great sacrifice has come on the heels of this revelation – from Moses to Christ. It also indicates that there is a great anointing upon it as well! What better way to receive the good that has been given to us by Christ than to denounce any association with those ungodly behaviors and stand fiercely in our true, scripturally sound identity.

PART II: SCRIBAL MINISTRY

"The secret things belong unto the Lord our God:
but those things which are revealed belong to us and to our children forever,
that we may do all the words of the Law."
~ Deuteronomy 29:29

PUBLISHING THE NEWS

The bible is an instruction manual for believers designed to teach them how to live a Christ-focused life, reconcile the lost and to make students of the Gospel.

In **Deuteronomy 32:2-4** Moses was shouting to the heavens and to the earth making declarations that exalted God and minimized himself. He shouted: *"My doctrine shall drop as the rain, my speech shall distil as the dew, as the small rain upon the tender herb, and as the showers upon the grass: **Because I will publish the name of the LORD: ascribe ye greatness unto our God.** He is the Rock, his work is perfect: for all his ways are judgments: A God of truth and without iniquity, just and right is he."*

Moses made it known to all within shouting range that he would live life *publishing* the name of the Lord and not his own doctrine or the doctrine of men.

I want you to look at the word "publish" for a moment. When Moses used this word, it was the first time "publish" in this sense was mentioned in the King James translation of the Bible. By contemporary definitions, publish is understood to mean to put something in print and distribute it to the public. Plain and simple. In Hebrew and within the context of its use here – it means so much more. The Strong's Concordance provides a range of meaning that includes to bear tidings, to announce, to bear news, to cause to hear, to tell, to proclaim, to sound aloud and even to be heard. In Greek, it means to herald, to foreshadow, to proclaim openly, to carry by different ways, to carry in different directions, to test, to prove by distinguishing between good and evil and to make matter.

Clearly, publishing is about way more than "putting something in print and distributing it publicly" as we have been taught in Babylon. As prophetic scribes, it is critical that our entire concept, perspective and insight shifts concerning the meaning of this word. Publishing is a state of being for the prophetic writer, prophetic scribe. Truly, the priestly scribes of old knew and lived these truths. Outside of knowing what it means to be a scribe instructed, I believe this is the next, most invaluable piece of knowledge and understanding that can be drawn from this book. We DESPERATELY need to know who we are. Ignorance is killing our scribal heritage.

Luke 12:47-49 says, *"And that servant who knew his master's will, and did not prepare himself or do according to his will, shall be beaten with many stripes. But he who did not know, yet committed things deserving of stripes, shall be beaten with few. For everyone to whom much is given, from him much will be required; and to whom much has been committed, of him they will ask the more."*

Let us take a very close look at the passage above. I want you to ask yourself this question, "Who is leading me?" There are only four possible answers to this question. Answer earnestly as you consider what you are learning about *The Scribal Anointing*®. The truth is, there are only four possible influences in your life:

- You are leading yourself.

- You are following the pattern and voice of others.
- You are following the ungodly spirit of this age.
- You are following the leading of Holy Spirit.

Luke 12:47-49 offers a great deal of wisdom for us to consider. It also clearly tells us that it is far better to do as the Spirit directs than to follow our own will. I have learned that most people are primarily under the influence of their "own mind" – not the adversary, other people or even the spirit of this age. The divided heart is at root in quite a bit of our situations and circumstances. This is why "being instructed" in the Kingdom of God is so extremely critical. Ignorance is no longer an excuse for missing the mark!

I have had many people tell me that they want more of Jesus. But when you look at their lives, they are not reading their word; there's no prayer life; they are neglecting solid fellowship… and there is definitely no room for accountability. Honestly, we can't "get more of Christ." We already have all of Him that we will ever need. The problem is that we need to posture ourselves to "recognize him" and "receive" all that He has for us. I'm not talking about material things here, but the kind of posturing that positions the soul for "spiritual maturity" and the unlocking of "deep things."

We do not want to be the rebellious believer who knew to do God's will, but chose our own way. Nor do we want to remain oblivious to God's will and pull out the "I didn't know card." Neither one, as we see here, is an adequate excuse. Why? Because when we enter the Kingdom, we enter with full access to Holy Spirit! He dwells with us and will not withhold ANY good thing from those who believe. Maturity must be sought after. Intimacy must be developed and then nurtured. It amazes me that the word "publish" has the same meaning in the day of Moses as it does today. We simply need to see it from all sides, not just the singular dimension of publishing a product, message or service. I pray you hear me.

This is, perhaps, the greatest pleas in this hour for prophetic scribes. From this point on, when you hear the word publish, I implore you to get "the world's definition" of publishing out of your mind. Take a look at the following bible verses on the next page that talk about *publishing* the word. Using the definitions provided early, please take the time to replace the word publish with each one of them so that you can see for yourself what God is commanding his prophetic scribes to do today. Take a look at these passages:

1 Samuel 31:9
*And they cut off his head, and stripped off his armour, and sent into the land of the Philistines round about, **to publish it in the house of their idols,** and among the people.*

Esther 1:22
*For he sent letters into all the king's provinces, into every province according to the writing thereof, and to every people after their language, that every man should bear rule in his own house, and that it should **be published according to the language** of every people.*

Esther 8:13

*The copy of the writing for a commandment to be given in every province **was <u>published</u> unto all people**, and that the Jews should be ready against that day to avenge themselves on their enemies.*

Psalm 68:11

*The Lord gave the word: great was **the company of those that <u>published</u> it.***

Isaiah 52:7

*How beautiful upon the mountains are the feet of him that bringeth good tidings, **that <u>publisheth</u> peace;** that bringeth good tidings of good **that <u>publisheth</u> salvation;** that saith unto Zion, Thy God reigneth!*

Jeremiah 4:16

*Make ye mention to the nations; **behold, <u>publish</u> against Jerusalem,** that watchers come from a far country, and give out their voice against the cities of Judah.*

Amos 4:5

*And offer a sacrifice of thanksgiving with leaven, **and proclaim and <u>publish</u>** the free offerings: for this liketh you, O ye children of Israel, saith the Lord GOD.*

Mark 5:20

*And he departed, and began **to <u>publish</u> in** Decapolis how great things Jesus had done for him: and all men did marvel.*

Mark 13:10

*And the gospel must first **be <u>published</u> among all nations.***

Luke 8:39

*Return to thine own house, and shew how great things God hath done unto thee. And he went his way, **and <u>published</u> throughout the whole city** how great things Jesus had done unto him.*

Acts 13:49

*And the word of the Lord <u>**was published**</u> throughout all the region*

If we are to really examine the making of a scribe, as we understand it to be in antiquity, we will quickly grasp that the first act of publishing wasn't the scrolls, parchments or prophecies at all. The first act of publishing is the life of the scribe itself – not the product or production. True scribes understand that THEY are God's first published Work, and that the condition of their hearts are the true publishing houses long before they produce their scribal projects. Point Blank: Publishing begins there. The scribal project is only a continuation of this truth.

WRITING THE PROPHETIC WORD OF THE LORD

The avenues and methods of communicating today have become instant and global. We have wireless technologies, multiple communication devices, and the world-wide web at our disposal. Plus, we still have the conventional methods of the past.

We are living in a time when a tremendous amount of focus has been placed on obtaining and accessing information quickly and accurately. In addition, technology has renewed the world's interest in reading and writing. More books are being printed than ever before – just look at the rise of audio books, e-books, e-libraries and the explosion of self-publishing. We can see that this growth is a direct result of living in a technology driven information age, and that God is positioning us for the fulfillment of prophecy – the reaching of the potential unreachable with the Gospel.

The bible speaks of the influx of information through books in **Ecclesiastes 12:11-13:** *"The words of the wise are like goads, and the words of the scholars are like well-driven nails, given by one Shepherd. And further my son be admonished by these.* ***Of making many books there is no end*** *and much study is wearisome to the flesh. Let us fear God and keep his commandments for this is man's all."*

King Solomon was prophesying when he wrote this passage. Even the literary genres are expanding and changing. The publishing industry has seen a huge jump in books of cultural, political and religious influence – so much so that in some areas the markets have tapped out. And our world, as we know it, is in a great battle concerning faith, morals and values. There was a time when I could go to a bookstore on any corner and head directly for the Christianity section, pick up what I needed, pay and leave. Today, I have to shift through the "Spirituality" section or take my chances at a "Christian" bookstore. The word "Christian" doesn't contain the meaning that it did just a decade ago. We must tune our hearts and minds into the times and seasons in which we live and to begin to grasp the critical role we play in it.

God is calling us to be light in the midst of darkness. He's calling us to be reflections of him, not mirror images of the political or cultural climate in which we live. When it comes to our Lord and Savior Jesus Christ, there's no such thing as being "politically correct." It's an issue of standing up for his word – no matter the cost.

You see, doors to communicate the word have opened that were previously closed. No longer are we at the mercy of agents, publishers, elite writing associations or publishing houses that dictate what is worth printing and what is not. No longer are we at the mercy of marketing and promotions companies, and advertisers who handpick their clientele. God has opened the doors to success. But we must be able to recognize those doors when they open.

Our time to walk through this door of opportunity for the creative, prophetic word of the Lord and impact God's Kingdom is *now*. The key is this: We must know how and when to use the tools that he has placed in our hands.

FACT: Prophetic scribes who write the creative word of the Lord are also worship arts ministers and/or leaders. Never, ever lose sight of this. It changes EVERYTHING about who you are.

Understanding the Prophetic Scribe

THE OFFICE OF
THE PROPHETIC SCRIBE

↓

WRITER
JOURNALIST
LAWYER
PUBLISHER
PRINTER
COPY EDITOR
ORATOR
JUDGE
TRANSCRIPTIONIST
CLERK
SECRETARY
DEVOTIONALIST
NOVELIST
NEWS REPORTER
COPYIST
TREASURER
(OTHER AREAS)

It is refreshing to bring a new perspective to this section of *The Scribal Anointing: Scribes Instructed in the Kingdom of Heaven.* Over the course of the past 10 years, my knowledge and understanding of the prophetic scribe has increased tremendously. Early, I stated emphatically that "prophetic writing" and the "prophetic scribe" are not exactly the same thing. We discussed that a *prophetic writer* is indeed a prophetic scribe; but a prophetic scribe is not necessarily a prophetic writer. Rather, the prophetic scribe is the umbrella under which we will find *all scribal functions,* including that of the prophetic writer.

To be a prophetic scribe is to walk in ANY FUNCTION of the prophetic scribe that falls within The Scribal Anointing®. The illustration to your left is designed to help put this in a simple, easy to understand perspective. Prayerfully, this dispels many of the failed definitions that are being purported across prophetic schools of ministry in this hour. As often as possible, I believe it is imperative that we bring this truth before all scribes who are willing listen – and not limit this calling to simply writing and recording. In addition, review the "Emergence of Scribal Ministry" chart that I shared with you earlier.

What does it mean to be prophetic?

So far, we have used the term "prophetic" without defining it. Before going any further, I need to provide a bare-bones definition of it for our purposes here. For the sake of keeping things simple for anyone who reads this book, I define the prophetic as the "gift bestowed upon believers by Holy Spirit that enables us to know and release the heart and mind of God."

Simple.

To the point.

To *be prophetic* for "the writer" can be viewed as the state of being filled with Holy Spirit and used by God to deliver a divine message or directive to others through your specific scribal gifting. A person who is prophetic can accurately convey or demonstrate God's will in the same or similar way that prophets did in the scripture. The word released or demonstrated is understood to be revelation or divine insight. What makes a believer a "prophetic writer" is not simply that they write, but that this is *the primary or chosen means* by which the Lord chooses to use them in ministry. I often tell people that if I am considered to walk in no other office in ministry or have any other calling on my life, no one would ever deny that I am a scribe. Why? I am ALWAYS immersed in some sort of scribal activity - especially writing. So not only am I understood to be a prophetic scribe, but I have a consistent track record of writing prophetically that spans nearly two decades. Without hesitation, I can declare myself a prophetic writer.

Acts 2 indicates that every believer has access to the gift of prophecy and has the God given ability to prophesy. Unfortunately, not every believer will walk in that gift (1 Corinthians 14:5). In the same way, not every believer who writes is a prophetic writer; any more than everyone who prophesies walks in the office of a prophet. They may be *prophetic*, and perhaps God has given them one or two scribal projects to complete - but writing a book or two, producing one or two plays doesn't make that person a prophetic writer or a prophetic scribe. Just as there are distinct signs of a prophet, apostle, pastor, etc. there are also distinct signs that identify a prophetic writer.

I have met many types of believers who write over the years. Some were inspired to write a particular item or complete a specific body of work (play, skit, monologue, etc.) and then, once that assignment was completed they would never have the desire, inspiration or inclination to produce anything scribal again. God simply needed them to fulfill that specific assignment and carry it forth. They would not necessary be considered a scribe or prophetic writer, but simply someone who had The Scribal Anointing® come upon them for that time. Writing a book and walking in the office of a prophetic scribe as a prophetic writer are two different things.

A person called to the office of a scribe will have a constant manifestation of the gifting or calling in their lives on a daily basis. Scribal activity will be their norm at every possible turn, and their hearts will be overcome with a great passion, zeal and urgency concerning that calling - whether God called them from their youth or they were suddenly activated one day years into adulthood.

Here are some signs of a prophetic scribe.

Signs of a Prophetic Scribe

I heard a preacher say this recently at a conference, "Every gift you have inside you is used to support your calling." When I heard this, I almost threw my purse down and began running across that room. It blessed me just that much!

To some people, this is not a big deal at all. But for me, it caused me to do an instant inventory of my life and come to one simple conclusion: "Every single gifting that I have demonstrated in my life LED ME directly into this calling as a prophetic scribe!" If I am nothing else by way of calling and purpose, I am clearly God's prophetic scribe who functions at a high level in the area of prophetic writing. What does this mean for you? It means that you might need to take an inventory of your gifts simply to see HOW they support the calling that is upon your life.

Below are a few signs of a prophetic writer. In reviewing them, I pray that you will recognize some of these characteristics in your own life. Prophetic writers:

- *Often pray, intercede or talk with God through their pen.* They tend to work out the issues of their heart in their notebooks or journals – sharing secret things that only God will hear. In this place, writing has become an ear and a tool used for self-deliverance, healing, impartation, contemplation, joy, building and adoration to the Father.

- *Write or record from a strong, unplanned or unrehearsed a flow.* The words simply stream from the Spirit of the Lord into their hearing and through their recording device or pen. This includes dialogue, novel scenes, songs, poetry, spoken word, the wording of letters, contracts, book content organization, etc.

- *Once awakened by the Lord, experience constant manifestations of their gifting.* In other words, they are daily operating in an aspect of their scribal function. This can be equated to the same level of passion one might see in a musician, psalmist or visual artist. The gifting literally begins to consume and shape their lives.

- *Have a pre-occupation with recording what they see, hear and/or experience from the Lord.* As the gift matures, they begin to experience a desire to share what they receive with others.

- *May have a special gift and anointing to hear and see stories, articles, novels and books in the lives of or on behalf of others.* They walk under a special grace in which they are primarily "recorders" in the Kingdom; and may or may not write or record extensively for themselves.

- *Experience a consistent urgency to release what they record.* This includes publishing blogs, books, videos, speaking or even by way of prophetic demonstration through plays, skits, monologues, movies, etc. Everything they release is always backed up so-to-speak as a record.

- *Are drawn to specific types of notebooks, pens, paper, ink types, ink color or other writing essentials – to a point of near obsession.* They are often adamant in what they record with, where they record, how they record and how their finished work is presented. For many of them, these are preferences they are not willing to shy away from.

- *Have an intense passion, love and respect for words - including how they are presented and how they impact the hearts of others.* It's not strange to see the scribe engrossed in word games, reading encyclopedias, dictionaries, taking frequent trips to the library, or other material that challenges the vocabulary.

- May have a passion for story-telling or recounting events from the unique biblically-sound, spiritual perspective God has given them – with a strong desire to preserve foundational biblical truths, family legacies, etc. This may also go hand in hand with a passion for parables and the passion for teaching.

- *May have the ability to decipher complicated documents, contracts, plans or letters with little or no effort, with or without prior training and regardless of the genre.* They have keen discernment and insight in this area for every assignment that is designed for them by the Lord.

- *May have the ability to write letters, administrative documents, contracts, poetry, skits, etc. without any significant effort.* Some scribes have an affinity toward perfection as it comes to spelling, grammar and presentation – to a point of extremes.

By no means is this a complete list of signs a prophetic writer might demonstrate, but it should put you on a path of considering the gifts that are evident in your life and those that are emerging. Scribal ministry UNFOLDS. It is not unusual for believers to exhibit only one or two signs and then at a later date observe others bursting forth! So don't get discouraged if you cannot relate to many of the bullet points above. In addition, I want to encourage you to purchase this book, "*40 Signs of a Prophetic Scribe,*" at your convenience.

Are You a Skilled Writer or a Prophetic Writer?

A *skilled writer*, as used here, is defined as someone who has been trained to write in a specific area of expertise based on techniques, standards, mechanics and best practices – whether it's a street style or professional study. This type of writer relies solely on intellect, training or technique and their own understanding to construct a work. Their inspiration may come from a very tangible, credible source and provide good information, but the efforts put into building that work is not divinely inspired. They have been taught by the world how to construct their projects as a writer and have become experts in doing so. In extreme cases, if a writing project doesn't meet certain standards or criteria based on academic or professional expectations, it is not considered "worthy" writing.

A *prophetic writer* is focused on receiving God's direction concerning what to put to paper. They are sensitive to the Spirit. They cannot sit and construct a literary work based solely on a thought or idea alone without strategic, supernatural direction. A prophetic scribe may author instructional materials (sermons, curriculums, self-help books, study guides, etc.), administrative materials (letters, documents, contracts, etc.) or they may write creative works (songs, poetry, spoken word, novels, memoirs, articles, short stories, novels, etc.) – without any specific training or technique in mind. The difference is this – prophetic is focused *exclusively* on what God is speaking into their spirit or what he is revealing to them for themselves or for others.

Is there something wrong with skilled writing? Absolutely not, as far as writing is concerned overall. But a prophetic writer places greater value on publishing the heart and mind of God. Skill and technique play an important role in this, but it does not supersede following God's lead. Sometimes, skilled writers completely ignore the leading of the Spirit and is only concerned with the structural outcome of the peace and the message with very little regard concerning how it will impact the Kingdom. That is the difference that is being pointed out here.

As a news reporter, I understand this very well. You are required to write in a specific format in many industries. As a result, I simply had to make sure the Lord was guiding my hand, perspective and insight as I did so. I had to literally give Holy Spirit permission to "stop my mind" from contemplating on sentence structure, spelling, grammar, writing techniques and styles (and so much more) – so that I could actually hear God and get what Father was saying "out of me." I had to PRAY, worship and intercede over my mind.

The merit of a *prophetic* piece of writing is judged on biblical soundness, spiritual discernment, impact, accurately conveying the heart and mind of God, and timing as it relates to the spiritual climate in which the piece was released and/or delivered. The presentation and structure of a work in this sense is critically important, but it would be secondary to getting that message written or recorded. My book, *Spiritually Critiquing Literary Works*, goes into great detail about this and is all about God's "merit system" verses that of the academic world.

The most important thing to remember here is that skilled writers and prophetic scribes *are not* necessarily the same. Prophetic scribes can *become* and *should* become skilled writers. I am convinced, however, that the principle needed in all of our lives is to first grasp hold of the spirit. In doing so, they are able to accurately employ our skills and abilities. **Operating solely in one area or the other is detrimental to our development!**

If you are a skilled scribe, give Holy Spirit permission to teach you to be a skilled *prophetic* scribe. If you are a prophetic scribe, ask Holy Spirit to lead you into courses or workshops where you can become a *skilled* prophetic scribe. Neither group can afford to ignore the fullness that both areas offer depending on your scribal assignment. Even as a grant writer who was prophetic, I had to learn how to "write grants" by taking courses through my employer at the time.

Proverbs 16:1-4 reads: "*The preparations of the heart belong to man, But the answer of the tongue is from the LORD. All the ways of a man are pure in his own eyes, But the LORD weighs the spirits. **Commit your works to the LORD, And your thoughts will be established.**"*

Developing a Teachable Spirit

Proverbs 18:12 CJB, *"A fool takes no pleasure in trying to understand; he only wants to express his own opinion."*

One of the most difficult challenges I have encountered in scribal ministry revolves around providing constructive criticism to prophetic people – especially prophetic writers. It is as if there is this mindset that declares: "God told me how to do it and how to write it, so I'm going to do it like this regardless of what anyone has to say." And sometimes, that "anyway" is a very, very bad representation of who God is. There is always room for improvement – especially in writing. We must remember that if God releases something to His people, He intends for them to get UNDERSTANDING.

Just because YOU understand what you wrote; does not mean that other people will!

There is no doubt that we are indeed commanded to obey God. But we are to do so in the midst of **common sense,** sensibility, order, practicality and excellence. God gave us our minds for a reason. Otherwise, we risk becoming fools and standing as a mockery before men; and adding to the plethora of things that shine a bad light in the midst of our faith. In scribal ministry specifically, this is just not a good place to be – especially if you are a scribe positioning yourself to publish, teach and lead others. Some of you know what I am speaking of because, like me, you have been in this place of knowing it all and rejecting sound counsel. I actually went through this phase! I took someone spelling it out to me before I really, really got it! I am thankful to God for his chastisement, patience and for saving me from myself. (I know some of you are joining me in saying, AMEN, as it relates to your own journey.)

Proverbs 15:22 CJB says, *"Without deliberation, plans go wrong; but with many advisers, they succeed."*

The term deliberation as used the Complete Jewish Bible version of **Proverbs 15:22** is powerful. It indicates the necessity of sometimes considering, contemplating, counting up the cost or otherwise thinking through a thing. The process of deliberation can require research, discussions, the reviewing of outlines and plans, or even receiving counsel. The phrase "many advisers" is not about random people; rather, it is about reaching into a circle of trust or within an area of expertise for guidance. After all, God's plan for wisdom involves not only drawing from Holy Spirit and reading our Word, but from one another and the resources around us.

Sometimes, prophetic people forget this.

Not everything drops out of the sky and into one's hands. There are many things we work toward and grow into learning. You see, a scribe may receive a spiritual download for a screen play but they need to know how to formally put a screen paper into a formatted manuscript if they are to be taken seriously. We cannot by-pass the professional process simply because "this is how I was told to do it or this is how I saw it in a dream."

People of God, we are not talking about changing the message of what you received. Rather, we are talking about organizing and presenting material in a way that others – besides you – know what is going on or taking place. This truth applies to every literary genre you can think of or imagine. Most people cannot submit a theatrical play to an agent in any-old-kind-of-format and expect those agents to follow what is going on in the manuscript; any more than you can submit a novel without character development, a setting or plot.

When I wrote my first book over decade ago, I did so from a place of spiritual vision while totally dismissing the practical. I closed my ear to anything and everything outside of "what I saw" – even when those who were spiritually sound and had professional experience above my pay-grade, so to speak, attempted to offer insight and help. I was too "spiritual" to listen and it cost me. Today, I'm rewriting several books – but this time I am doing so amid sound advice. I am walking it out from a humble, crushed place.

You can take those necessary steps of humility now; so you don't have to later!

When prophetic scribes fail to listen, they end up releasing projects that are mediocre or outright embarrassing instead of releasing their greatness. Small beginnings do not equal poor or deprived beginnings. We must always start with what we have. What is being conveyed here is the necessity of giving your best while also recognizing that you might need help.

Proverbs 4:6 CJB, *"Don't abandon [wisdom]; then she will preserve you; love her, and she will protect you."*

Humble yourself. Choose wisdom.

Passion, Urgency & Scribes

I cannot conclude our conversation surrounding "understanding the prophetic scribe" without addressing three additional elements of the calling: passion, zeal and urgency. I believe it is imperative that every prophetic writer allow Holy Spirit to cultivate these three areas in your life. In my journey, they have been critical catalysts in keeping me from growing weary in the midst of my journey. They stand with me to build endurance and to keep my heart firmly rooted in faith and hope.

I believe they will do the same for you. This ministry is not always celebrated or taken seriously. Those who find themselves in the trenches of any kind of scribal function should seek to gain their strength from these three areas.

Passion

Many of us would agree that there are very few things in life that we are passionate about. For me, my love of Christ is at the very top of that list. There is absolutely no doubt that those who love him fall into that category of "being a fool for Christ" as described by the Apostle Paul in **1 Corinthians 4:10**. Passion, from this perspective, reminds me of how King David nearly danced out of His clothes and how the apostles, and countless other martyrs, thought it was an honour to be crucified for Christ's sake. In consideration of these examples, passion has a dual meaning in the midst of our faith. On one hand, we have this unquenchable enthusiasm for Christ and on the other we have the Greek meaning of the word which means to "suffer with."

Clearly the scribes of old demonstrated this.

Clearly the scribes whom Christ declared would be flogged in the streets by those who hate the Gospel message; and those who would be murdered between the temple and the altar like Zacharias grasped what that meant. The point here is simple: Every prophetic scribe, prophetic writer must be prepared to embrace the level of passion required to fulfill their calling.

Romans 8:17 KJV says, *"And if children, then heirs; heirs of God, and joint-heirs with Christ; if so be that we suffer with him, that we may be also glorified together."*

Urgency

There is also a level of "urgency" that walks hand-in-hand with scribal ministry. Recognizing, embracing and responding to this urgency ensures that we fulfill our ministry and do not become stagnant. This is an area that can be cultivated and strengthened if we allow Holy Spirit to lead and guide us.

I define urgency as an overwhelming "immediacy" that comes upon by Holy Spirit. Nearly every prophetic scribe will experience an urgency to not only write, record or demonstrate – but to publish or otherwise release or demonstrate what they have been given. **I must note, however, that urgency in the realm of the spirit and urgency in the natural are two different things.** The first lines up with the prompting of the spirit to fulfill Kingdom matters in timely matter; or the prompting to take care of critical time-sensitive situations in the natural that reflects proper stewardship. In this sense, spiritual and natural deadlines are made clear.

The second type of urgency is "rushing" and has the potential to spin one's projects and life out of control. We want to avoid this! As scribes, we want to fulfill our assignments from a place of spiritual urgency or stewarding deadlines in the natural. As we mature in discernment, Holy Spirit teaches us how to recognize our own spiritual alarm clock and specific times to release what God gives us.

Jeremiah 20:9 AMP says, *"If I say, I will not make mention of [the Lord] or speak any more in His name, in my mind and heart it is as if there were a burning fire shut up in my bones. And I am weary of enduring and holding it in; I cannot [contain it any longer]."*

Ezra exemplified both of these in His scribal ministry, and they enabled Him to endure, to finish His race.

Writing from Your Five-Fold Office

Ephesians 4:11 AMP reads, *"And he gave some, apostles; and some, prophets; and some, evangelists; and some, pastors and teachers; For the perfecting of the saints, for the work of the ministry, for the edifying of the body of Christ…"*

In my personal journey as a scribe, I spent many nights being jolted awake by the Lord in the middle of the night then clamoring for pen, paper or digital recorder to write down the streams of poetry or prophecy flowing from my spirit. This was not just a random act, but a nightly occurrence that went on for years.

In the beginning, most of my writing came in poetic form and carried a familiar theme of prayers, declarations and personal prophecy concerning myself. As I matured, those encounters began changing drastically. The poetic flow was more akin to poetic prophecy, direct prophecy and prophetic teaching through monologues, plays and skits. I would literally take these treasures from my dream realm, post them on my blog, take them to an open mic or turn them into poetic plays or skits at God's leading. Quite honestly, I simply walked out the instructions I believe Holy Spirit was pouring into me. Because I had such a passion for scribal ministry, I never questioned what I was doing or even why. I just knew the Lord had placed these things in my heart and I had to present them before those who would listen. My mentor at that time would review quite a bit of my writings and would identify many of them as prophetic words and prophesies for the local congregation and the Body of Christ. It was then that I began to realize that I had moved from the prophetic into the realm of prophecy. What was even more unusual to me at the time was that my poetic messages and prophecies always seemed to target a specific group of people or issue affecting the global congregation, especially in the area of healing through worship and the arts.

I had advanced from simply writing prophetically to operating in the office of a prophet. Within two years, I had gone through intensive training in a School of the Prophets; was ordained as a prophet, and licensed into ministry through a local congregation. It was from this point forward that I became acutely aware of how the ministry of "prophetic writing" could be amplified through the **Ephesians 4:11** callings of apostle, prophet, evangelist, pastor and teacher.

Understanding this is simple. You see, mature ministers will automatically write, record or demonstrate their scribal ministry within the confines of their calling. Their pen will simply carry their voice. In other words, those same characteristics that cause mature ministers to recognize when an apostle, prophet, evangelist, pastor or teacher is in their midst will flow just as profoundly through their scribal ministries.

On a very basic level, we might see consistent patterns in the life of a scribe that might line up with what is presented in the list below:

- **The Scribal Apostle.** Those walking in this office will pioneer new ideas, define and implement strategies, usher in fresh understanding and reformation in key areas. They will bring order and alignment in their area of specialty, fortify Christ's foundations, challenge and disrupt old manmade patterns, continuously preach Christ crucified and martial the people of God toward progression and reformation. **(Galatians 1:13-16; Acts 1:8-10)**

- **The Scribal Prophet.** Those walking in this office will be the mouthpiece of Christ in the earth – upholding the foundations of faith; directing, correcting, equipping and strengthening the Body; and speaking into the destiny of the people of God that they may be covered for the works of darkness. **(Jeremiah 1:8-10; Acts 21:10; Ephesians 2:20)**

- **The Scribal Evangelist.** Those walking in this office will consistently release a cry that longs to see Father's people saved. **(Romans 10:1; Phil 1:7)**

- **The Scribal Pastor.** Those walking in this office will consistently release messages that feed, guide, lead, **nurture, encourage and mature** the sheep. **(Acts 20:28; 1 Peter 5:2)**

- **The Scribal Teacher**. Those walking in this office will consistently release practical application of the word with a desire to see Father's people reach understanding. **(Acts 11:26; Hebrews 5:12).**

As prophetic scribes mature (growing in their ability to live holy lives, hear, understand and obey Father), they may find themselves exhibiting signs of these areas of ministry. **However, it is important to remember that God does not bestow an "office or seat of authority" upon anyone who lacks the character, self-control and love of God to be a good custodian over it.** Walking in the "gift" is not enough to take a seat in the office. That is the equivalent of trying to fly a plane as a "pilot" because you read the book and took a class. A pilot who is ready to fly must also log a certain number of flight hours while submitted to an actual instructor before graduating to that level and being trusted with hundreds of lives on a plane.

We live in a time when people "see a gift in operation" and they think they are ready to lead in the gift. This is a gross misconception, especially when that person has not come up in the ranks OR does not exemplify the character of God in a stable, mature place in that office. It would be unwise for me to include the details above without also sharing this aspect as well. Finally, don't be in a hurry to take a position or move into an office. Just allow God to have His perfect work in the midst of your scribal ministry. Remember, everything is beautiful in its time.

In the workshops and classes that we teach, we go through each of these areas in great detail. In addition, there are more defined books available to help you walk through each of these areas.

Writing & Recording Prophetic Words

These days, every one with a prophetic school or who hosts a prophetic writing class believes they know how to properly "write" a prophetic word or a prophecy that you may receive from the Lord. The truth is, there is no single formula for doing this - especially since many prophetic writers are rappers, psalmists, poets and spoken word artists. If what God has given you is a poetic prophecy, song or rap, then how you write or record it is specifically associated with your writing style. And no one can police that but Holy Spirit! Most prophetic writers will walk in that place of releasing exhortation, encouragement, comfort or other areas that build the Body of Christ.

Our prophetic words could be in the form of:
- Prayers
- Poetry, Spoken Word, Rap
- Plays, Skits, Monologues or other forms of demonstration
- Rap, Song
- Letters, Written Prophecies
- Declarations, Decrees
- Parables, including varying scripts
- Dreams, Visions
- Prophetic demonstrations, teachings

Yes, I know this is a broad list. I believe, however, we have done a disservice to the prophetic by limiting it only to those things surrounding "the Lord is saying." I believe we have direct prophecy, of which most people are familiar with especially orally, and then prophecy through expanded written and recorded forms. **Scribal ministry compels us to realize that the release of prophecy can take on many, many forms.** The writing and demonstrating prophets and prophetic people of the Bible demonstrate this.

I want to encourage you to be bold! Take a chance. Obviously, you MUST deliver the Word God gives you in love. This doesn't mean compromise as so many believers think when you use that term. The best way I know to describe this to you is that there is no need to be harsh, mean or judgmental in your delivery. No prophecy should follow behind a nasty attitude. I must insist that you read **Ephesian 4** in its entirety using a solid bible like the New King James Version or the Amplified. Pay close attention to the last six or seven verses of that passage; then follow it up with **1 Corinthians 13**.

Do not be fearful.

Nearly everyone whom God uses to write, record, orate or otherwise deliver a prophetic word has experienced fear of some kind. I'm not going to give you a bunch of scriptures about overcoming fear. Most of us are aware of those. I will say, however, that being courageous in releasing what God gives you will position you to overcome fear. Part of this bold, strategic walk as scribes will require walking through the criticism and judgment of others concerning what you write, record or release. It will require being in a position to defend or stand for what Holy Spirit releases through you. This is the normal, everyday experience for prophetic writers in general – not just those who are releasing prophetic words. Also realize that no matter how "spiritual or seasoned" you think you may be, people do make mistakes and miss God. NO ONE is immune from the influence of fear or haughtiness; nor has anyone gotten it right every single time. The mere fact that making a statement like this angers some who are reading it, speaks of the need to receive a greater level of humility. We can walk in humility if our only motive is making Christ known and glorifying His Word, will and way.

Everyone walks through times in which they fail to accurately discern and distinguish:
- The voice of God;
- The voice of God from their voice;
- The voice of God from the many voices and echoes that enter their hearing;
- The voice of God from religious or legalistic ideals that they have believed;
- The voice of God from bad teaching or poor understanding of scripture; and
- The voice of God from the voice of compromise;
- The voice of God from the voice of the adversary.

"Ain't no shame in telling the truth," as the old people used to say. There are even times when some prophetic scribes struggle to hear God! Let's be truthful here! There are legitimate struggles that prophetic people face every day in their receiving and delivering of God's Word. Even in this, we *overcome* in the midst of our pursuit. We learn to hear Him clearly! We pursue, press and walk it out! My own testimony is one riddled with mistakes, chastisement, redirection, being broken… and ultimately learning to submit and trust God. Even now – in this mature place, I seek out accountability and counsel. I can remember releasing prophetic words from a very religious place. With proper training, guidance and the patience of mentors, I overcame.

Don't get discouraged in YOUR process. God uses every single thing we conquer for His glory. He uses our weaknesses for our learning; and teaches us to recognize and receive His strength. I want to challenge you not to be TOO HARD ON YOURSELF. I want you to be so rooted in the Lord and in touch with Holy Spirit that you will be extremely wise in releasing prophetic words. Let the fear of the Lord have its perfect work in your heart!

Next, allow the Lord to develop your unique voice and method(s) of delivery. You do not have to sound like everyone else. Before I provide you with some practical insight on writing and recording prophecy, I need to highlight three things:

1) **You must become a lover of the written Word of God.** Allow Holy Spirit to give you a passion to read, <u>study</u> and rightly divide its truths. This is non-negotiable. Never has there been a prophet OR SCRIBE in the history of the scriptures that was not intimately and deeply acquainted with God's Word. ***Don't fall into the deception of thinking you are the exception to this truth.*** Also, study from a solid bible version that is translated as closely as possible from the original Hebrew and Greek. Many of the Bibles today lack content that can be properly studied out.

2) **You must have a solid prayer lifestyle.** I didn't say prayer life here, but *lifestyle*. Prayer, and all of its facets, is the most intimate expression of relationship with God that anyone can have outside of reading the Word! This includes intercession, warfare and especially confession of sin and repentance.

3) **Be accountable in the prophetic.** Every prophetic Word should be judged. No prophetic person is above this truth… *ever.*

I must tell you that anyone who seeks to prophesy without rooting their lives in the Word and in prayer are subject to *extreme* error, ungodly influence and great deception. Period. **Scribes of old remained inside the Word.** Believers who ignore these requirements often move into grave areas of carnality and witchcraft within the prophetic. Don't be that person!

When writing and recording prophecy:

- Make sure the prophecy lines up with the Word, works and ways of Christ. **(John 12:49)**

- Have the Word judged by mature prophets and apostles just as you would a spoken prophecy – especially when you are learning. **(1 Thessalonians 5:12; 1 Corinthians 14:29; Jeremiah 28:5-9)**

- Make sure the prophetic word is clear for those who read it. Not only does it need to be well written, but it must also be understandable. If neither of those things are possible, don't post it. Understanding is one of the most critical aspects of releasing a prophetic Word. Just because YOU understand it does not mean that other's will.

- You do not *have to* note every single line of the prophetic word with a scripture. Many people do this, and nothing is wrong with it per se. However, if Holy Spirit has not expressly directed you to release your prophetic words this way…then do not do it simply because someone else does.

- Date the prophetic words you release. This can serve multiple purposes, especially when prophesying into specific events, occurrences, etc.

- Sign your name or state that you wrote it. Most people love giving "anonymous" words as some spiritual act when in truth, they are avoiding accountability and challenges that may come. If you do this, please be sure that your motives are RIGHT in seeking to be anonymous. Most prophets in scripture associated themselves with the Words they released.

- Do not speak or write in "King James English." Trust me, God did not speak like this. There's no reason for you to either. It is a religious, learned behaviour. It can be a huge distraction to your reader, listener or viewer... unless it is a part of the "creative delivery" of your prophetic word... like in a play or skit.

Is God Speaking?

Briefly, I must answer one of the most common questions I receive from scribes who are growing in the prophetic: How do I know if God is speaking? Or how can I learn to hear from the Lord? The answer to this question is not as complicated as one might think.

First, let's take a look at John 10:27 which says, *"My sheep listen to my voice, I recognize them, they follow me..."*

The most important thing to remember about hearing God or recognizing His voice is to first "assess your position" in Him. In this passage, Christ declares that those who *know* Him can *hear* Him. Step one, if we can use steps, is making sure that you fall in the "sheep" category. I believe a thorough picture has been presented of what sheep (or sons) look like... especially as we unveiled the Ezra Pattern. Secondly, Christ gives us an amazing clue in **John 12:49**. He says, *"I have not spoken on My own, but the Father who sent Me has commanded Me what to say and how to say it..."*

One of the primary ways we can know if God is speaking is by "knowing the Word of God," particularly reading the New Covenant and the words that were spoken by Christ and later by His apostles. From this, we can conclude that God will NEVER contradict His Word either through logos or rhema. The passage below summarizes this.

2 Timothy 3:16: *"All Scripture is God-breathed and is useful for teaching, rebuking, correcting and training in righteousness."*

Finally, we can measure our hearing by clearly grasping what is on the HEART of God. Yes, God hates sin. But he LOVES people – and I am not speaking of a fleshly love, but one in which HE GIVES UP ON NO ONE and meets them with that intent. It's people who give up on Him, and turn away from Him. What does this mean for us? It means that when He speaks, all roads will leave back to his singular desire: "To see men reconciled back to Him." Every word of correction that poured from the mouth of Christ and those who followed his pattern was one in which HE RELEASED GOD'S WILL and DEALT WITH ANY HINDRANCE to His will going forth. This doesn't mean that everything we write must reflect scriptures word-by-word like a robot. It does mean that we are continuing to carry that message of becoming one with God and forsaking all that stands in the way of our reconciliation.

Also remember that God's word gives life! It will never, ever make provision for a man's flesh, specifically giving men permission to sin. God's Word will benefit His congregation according to His will – without exception.

Romans 13:14 says: *"But put on the Lord Jesus Christ, and **make no provision for the flesh, to fulfill its lusts.**"*

2 Peter 3:8-9 says, *"But do not forget this one thing, dear friends: With the Lord a day is like a thousand years, and a thousand years are like a day. The Lord is not slow in keeping his promise, as some understand slowness. Instead he is patient with you, not wanting anyone to perish, but everyone to come to repentance."*

From the age of six to nine, I spent a great deal of time with my mother. I knew the sound of her footsteps, her smell and could identify her mood by the pitches in her voice. By the time I was an adult, I knew her so well that I could predict her responses or reactions to situations long before I brought them to her attention. Well, for those who claim to have an intimate relationship with Father we should know what is pleasing to Him – even to this degree. We should know His tenor, the fragrance of His anointing. All of his sons, intimately, have this kind of access to Him. We, however, simply have to put in the time needed to develop this kind of intimacy. Finally, I'd like to add that God's heart, mind and will are always reflective of His Word. This simply means that anything we hear should completely line up with what we read in His Word, especially those things revealed through the life of Jesus Christ.

I can't say this enough: *If the Word is not being poured into your spirit, then there is no way it's going to come out of your spirit. If you're not spending time reading, studying, praying and meditating on the Word, then you won't grow to recognize His voice when he speaks.*

God speaks to us in multiple ways. As you read the Bible, you will become acquainted with those ways and be better prepared to receive His voice. This is so important. He may speak through clear streaming thoughts or in an audible voice (**Genesis 6:13-21; Genesis 4:6; Revelations 1:10**), visions and dreams (**Genesis 37:9**, **Matthew 27:19**, **Acts 10:3**), the scriptures (**2 Timothy 3:16**), other people (**Acts 9:9-11**, **1 Samuel 7:2-4**) and even through preaching, angelic encounters, impressions, circumstances and situations.

Obviously, we know that God would never tell us to hate, hold grudges, ignore people, do evil or commit evil acts, harm ourselves or harm others. His voice will always lead to paths of repentance, forgiveness, brotherly love, serving, helping others or other life giving principles revealed through Christ. You don't have to fear "hearing Him." Rather, trust Holy Spirit to guide you.

PART III: TRANSFORMING YOUR MINISTRY

"Let this mind be in you which was also in Christ Jesus, who, being in the form of God, did not consider it robbery to be equal with God, but made Himself of no reputation, taking the form of a bondservant, and coming in the likeness of men. And being found in appearance as a man, He humbled Himself and became obedient to the point of death, even the death of the cross."
~ Philippians 2:5-8

AUTHENTIC TRANSFORMATION

There are three things a prophetic writer must do to tap into the depths of *The Scribal Anointing*®. With Holy Spirit's guidance, we must:

1. Forget everything the world has taught us about writing and being a scribe.

2. Concentrate all efforts on building a personal relationship with Christ through prayer and studying the Word.

3. Make sure you are fellowshipping with strong, Christ-centered believers who live what they teach and seek to walk in the way of the Word.

If a scribe can move forward in these three areas of their lives, then they are well on the way to building their scribal ministries on solid ground instead of on shifting sand. The greatest obstacle prophetic scribes and other worship arts ministers face today is that many *chase the gift and its benefits as they see it* and *not* the Father. It's critical that we follow Ezra's example.

Let's take a closer look at the three points mentioned:

1. **Forget everything the world has taught you about writing.** The first step is mind renewal – the putting on of the mind of Christ. Again, ask the Holy Spirit to take away those things you learned from the world about writing or walking as a scribe that will block your ability to hear divine instructions from God and prevent you from moving freely in the call upon your life. Then ask him to perfect your heart for the Kingdom purposes.

   The sooner the strongholds are broken the better. In the world, I was taught that certain things had to be in place before I could publish a book. Yes, I knew God wanted me to move forward with this book, but every time I sat down to write my mind went back to steps I'd been given in classes on the fundamentals of editing and how to get published. I spent more time researching resources than I did writing. All I could think about was finding an editor, designing the book cover, etc.

   One day I became extremely frustrated. So I asked God, *"Why isn't all of this stuff falling in place for me?"* Then I heard a plain and simple response, *"Theresa, all I told you to do was write the book."* That is all he said to me. I did not feel very intelligent at that moment. There I was telling others what to do and I was on my way to missing God. At that moment, I repented and realigned my thought life to my Father. I found a prophetic flow and churned out this book in less than five days. The more I wrote the more God poured into me. Later,

I realized that it was not up to me to meet my publishing needs; but it was up to God and God alone. This was HIS project – not mine. I found that once I got everything out of my spirit, I was able to go back and take an organized approach to putting everything together using some things I learned from the world.

Another perspective to consider is this.

I've always loved writing poetry. What I wrote was inspired by my personal pain and crafted by technique. An instructor told me that a couple of poems I wrote contained elements of "good writing" and I won a contest or two. But, my focus at that time was on making the poem look good, sound good and standout.

I was concerned about personal recognition and literary merit. Impact – in the spiritual sense - was never even a thought in my mind. As long as the piece was well written and the editors liked it, I was okay with that. My attitude was rooted in the mechanics of the writing and the response I wanted to evoke.

Well, writing for our Lord has nothing to do with technique and mechanics. It has everything to do with accurately conveying the heart of God. I learned quickly that I was supposed to critique writing for soundness of doctrine, the presence of the fruit of the spirit, and the ability of a piece to encourage, edify, comfort or otherwise exalt the body and draw men to the Father - *first*. Once those areas were solid, then the Lord would allow me to go back and check the other area.

We must be balanced in all that we do, not overly spiritual and grossly under skilled; or expertly skilled and lacking the ability to hear God's voice or recognize it when it is read on paper. I often tell writers that when your motives are correct and your heart is lined up with God, your priority will be to (1) Be aligned with the spirit realm first; and (2) focus on perfecting the skills and technique to present excellence. I tell you, this will only matter if the writer's focus in on God. Otherwise, this message will not penetrate the heart with understanding. Take a look at these scriptures:

John 7:17 says, *"If anyone wills to do His will, he shall know concerning the doctrine, whether it is from God or whether I speak on My own authority."*

John 7:16 says, *"...my doctrine is not mine, but he who sent me."*

Romans 12:12 says, *"And do not be conformed to this world, but be transformed by the renewing of your mind, that you may prove what is that good and acceptable and perfect will of God."*

2. **Concentrate all efforts on building a personal relationship with Christ through prayer and the word.** The word of God can't flow from you, if the word of God isn't flowing in and through you. You can achieve this personal relationship by:

   a. *Consistently studying the Word of God for understanding through revelation.* We talked about this in the previous section. Stressing it again should indicate to you just how important this step is in the midst of your life. Going to church and hearing a preacher is NOT enough. If you spend time in the word of God, then the Word will reveal itself in your writing. If you spend a little time in the Word, then a little Word will show itself in your writing. If you never spend time in the word of God, you will definitely release a mixture of things in your writing – especially your own thoughts, opinions and influences.

   2 Timothy 2:14-15 says, *"Remind them of these things, charging them before the Lord not to strive about words to no profit, to the ruin of the hearers. Be diligent to present yourself approved to God, a worker who does not need to be ashamed, rightly dividing the word of truth."*

   b. *In addition to studying, prayer is at the root of building this relationship.* This is another point we discussed in the previous section. Prayer is your direct line of communication with God, and the number one way to become familiar with His voice, heart and mind outside of reading the Word.

   The bible tells us that we should *"pray always with all prayer and supplication in the Spirit being watchful to this end with all perseverance and supplication for the saints – and for me that utterance may be given unto me that I may open my mouth boldly to make known the mystery of the gospel ..."* --**Ephesians 6:17-19.**

   Also **Philippians 4:6-7** says, *"Be anxious for nothing, but in everything by prayer and supplication, with thanksgiving, let your requests be made known to God; and the peace of God, which surpasses all understanding, will guard your hearts and minds through Christ Jesus."*

   After you pray, don't just get up and run off. Sit a while with your pen and notebook, ask the Holy Spirit some questions, and allow him to speak to your heart.

3. **Make sure you are accountable to others who can sharpen your gift, live for Christ and help you apply the Word in a practical way.** Being in accountability at a local church or with leadership that births submission, obedience, breeds a teachable spirit, provides

protection, and encouragement are invaluable. Iron sharpens iron! Truly you will grow and develop at a greater pace in the midst of fellowship with like-minded believers.

The bible says in **Romans 10:14**, *"How then shall they call on Him in whom they have no believed? And how shall they believe in Him of whom they have not heard? And how shall they hear without a preacher?"*

Jeremiah 3: 15 states plainly: *"And I will give you shepherds according to My heart who will feed you with knowledge and understanding."*

Hebrews 10:24-25 says, *"And let us consider one another in order to stir up love and good works, not forsaking the assembling of ourselves together, as is the manner of some, but exhorting one another, and so much the more as you see the Day approaching."*

YOUR GIFT DOES NOT DEFINE YOU

There are many believers who identify themselves by their talents and gifts. **This isn't good.**

This is no different from people who identify themselves by what they do on the job or by credentials, what they have, etc. At one point in my walk with God, I was consumed by my gift and I identified myself by my profession, talents and skills. If someone had asked me who I was, I would have immediately began telling them about what I did for a living or what I did in ministry. At one point in my scribal journey, I was so caught up in being a poet and spoken word artist that it became all that people saw. Then one day, I realized that whenever people called on me to minister – they only wanted the poet. At first I was outraged. I had the nerve to ask God, "Why doesn't anyone see that there's more to me than just poetry?" He responded: "That is how you present *yourself* and it is a reflection of how you have limited yourself in the things I have placed inside you. Your *entire* identity, daughter, is wrapped up in this gift."

Humph, I couldn't believe it. It wasn't about people. It was about me. I was limiting my own potential. I was trusting in a gifting and in a calling, not in God. I would even find myself extremely frustrated when I couldn't perform or receive new *material*. I saw it as God forsaking me instead of recognizing God was really trying to "awaken me" to what had become idol worship. Scribes of the King, it is so easy to move from pure ministry to worshipping a gift! We must come to a point in our walk in which our gifts and talents ARE NOT our identity. Rather, they are tools to help us fulfill our calling as disciples. Jesus' life stood on its own merit. So when he asked his disciples, *"Who do you say that I am?"* The Holy Spirit revealed the answer to Peter who said, "You are the Christ, the Son of the Living God." Take a look at this passage of scripture:

2 Corinthians 5:12-17 says: *"For we do not commend ourselves again to you, but give you opportunity to boast on our behalf, that you may have an answer for those who boast in appearance and not in heart. For if we are beside ourselves, it is for God; or if we are of sound mind, it is for you. For the love of Christ compels us, because we judge thus: that if One died for all, then all died; and He died for all, that those who live should live no longer for themselves, but for Him who died for them and rose again.*

Therefore, from now on, <u>we regard no one</u> according to the flesh. *Even though we have known Christ according to the flesh, yet now we know Him thus no longer. Therefore, if anyone is in Christ, he is a new creation; old things have passed away; behold, all things have become new."*

When we worship or gifts, then we become performers – not ministers. Please note that when I say this, I am not talking about the profession you may find yourself in at any given time or the environments you are called to minister within. I am speaking of a performance-mindset. There is a difference. Prophetic scribes must remain in the business of guarding their hearts and existing in the Spirit. (See the chart on the next page, "My Identity in Christ.")

Your Identity in Christ

MY RELATIONSHIP	MY POSITION
I'm a child of God - He is my Father - 1 John 3:1,2	I am connected to the true vine - John 15:1,5
I am Christ's friend - John 15:15	I'm a slave of righteousness - Romans 6:18, 22
I am born of God - 1 John 4:7	I am a temple of God - 1 Corin. 3:16; 6:19
I have been adopted by God - Romans 8:15	I am one spirit with the Lord - 1 Corin. 6:17
MY INHERITANCE	I am a member of Christ's body - 1 Corin. 12:27
I am an heir of God - Romans 8:17	I am reconciled to God - 2 Corin. 5:18
I am a joint heir with Christ - Romans 8:17; Gal. 4:7	I am a saint - Eph. 1:1; 1 Corin. 1:2; Phil. 1:1
I am blessed with every spiritual blessing - Eph. 1:3	I am a fellow citizen in God's Kingdom - Eph. 2:19
I am a child of the promise - Romans 9:8; Gal. 3:14	I have been brought near to Christ - Eph. 2:13
I've been given great promises - 2 Peter 1:4	I'm to be righteous and holy like God - Eph. 4:24
MY TRANSFORMATION	I have direct access to God - Eph. 2:18
I'm redeemed and forgiven - Eph. 1:6-8	I am a citizen of heaven - Phil. 3:20
I've been justified - made righteous - Romans 5:1	I've been rescued from Satan's domain - Col. 1:13
I have eternal life - John 5:24	I am hidden with Christ in God - Col. 3:3
I died w/Christ to the power of sin - Romans 6:1-6	I am chosen of God - holy, beloved - Col. 3:12
I am free from condemnation - Romans 8:1	I am a child of light, not darkness - 1 Thess. 5:5
I have received the Spirit of God - 1 Corin. 2:12	I am a partaker of Christ - Heb 3:14
I have been given the mind of Christ - 1 Corin. 2:16	I'm one of God's living stones - 1 Peter 2:5
I have been crucified with Christ - Gal. 2:20	I'm a member of a royal priesthood - 1 Peter 2:9
I am a new creation - 2 Corin. 5:17	I'm to be a stranger to this world - 1 Peter 2:11
I have received fullness in Christ - Col. 2:1	I'm an enemy of the devil - 1 Peter 5:8
MY CALLING	I am a partaker of a heavenly calling - Heb. 3:1
I am to be salt on the earth - Matt. 5:13	
I am to be light in the world - Matt. 5:14	
I'm chosen and appointed to bear fruit - John 15:16	
I am called to do the works of Christ - John 14:12	
I am to do what Christ commanded - Matt. 28:20	
I have been given spiritual authority - Luke 10:19	
Signs should accompany my work - Mark 16:17-20	
I am a minister of a new covenant - 2 Corin. 3:6	
I am a minister of reconciliation - 2 Corin. 5:18,19	
I am to be an expression of life in Christ - Col. 3:4	*This chart is used with written permission from Spiritual Warfare Ministries Online founder Donald Rogers, who is the founder.*

THE PURPOSE OF SCRIBAL MINISTRY

Have you ever thought about what it means to be a minister? I mean have you *really* thought about it. To *minister* means to be a servant to others and to wait upon them. Somewhere down the line the body of Christ walked into a place of confusion and misguidance in this area. Some people think it means *to be served* or to be entitled to some special treatment.

Our level of *"service to others"* increases with every promotion or elevation God gives us – in the natural or in the spirit. Many miss this revelation. I know I did. Take it from someone who has walked down that road, you *don't* want to be in place of pride and then have to have God snatch you down.

I can only imagine how wonderful it would be if everyone could be as excited about God as they would be if they won the Georgia Lottery jackpot. Hear me in the spirit when I say this, "The gift may be phenomenal to hear or read or see performed? The words penned on pages or shouted over an open mic may rile one audience or bring another to tears. You may find yourself on the road traveling here and there and being in high demand. But when all is said and done, God is still going to be looking at your heart? Our reflection must be a reflection of our Father.

Your Scribal Ministry

Let's just face the facts. Ministry in the body of Christ is all about reconciliation. There is absolutely no way around it. When Jesus commissioned his disciples to go and make disciples of all nations, he was expecting them to make full proof of their ministries. Our purpose is to become vessels on earth that exist solely to be used by God. Though we have different functions in the body, we share a singular purpose.

2 Corinthians 5:17-19 reads, *"Therefore, if anyone is in Christ he is a new creation; old things have passed away; behold all things have become new. Now all things are of God, who has reconciled us to Himself through Jesus Christ, **and has given us the ministry of reconciliation**, that is, that God was in Christ reconciling the world to Himself, not imputing their trespasses to them, and has committed to us the word of reconciliation."*

When I began writing prophetically, I heard a new voice rise inside me. I was amazed and elated that God could speak so clearly and loudly within my spirit. Everything in and of my life began to change as I became a new creation. The Holy Spirit caused me to express this new phase of my life through poetry. I didn't realize it then, but as I look back at my early writings, I can see that God was using my poetic gift to break strongholds in my life and declare victory in and through me over my circumstances. He was reconciling the "inner Theresa" back to him. Somewhere inside me, I knew that I would use the same words that restored me to usher restoration into the hearts of others. I felt like David who lamented often before the Lord with pen and paper in hand. Today, the songs that brought him reconciliation also brought it to countless men and women globally over centuries.

As I met other writers, I quickly learned that the prophetic gift within them was often stirred in the midst of a personal battle or crisis as well. God was using their situation to bring forth intercession, affirmation, encouragement and comfort to the body. One day the Lord said to me "Beloved, your pain and disappointment is someone else's healing and deliverance."

In that one sentence, the reality of **2 Corinthians 5:17-19** presented itself to me like a neon sign. From that point forward I wrote every word he gave me eagerly and with expectation.

Matthew 25:35-40 says, *"For I was hungry and you gave Me food, I was thirsty and you gave Me something to drink, I was a stranger and you brought Me together with yourselves and welcomed and entertained and lodged Me, I was naked and you clothed Me, I was sick and you visited Me with help and ministering care, I was in prison and you came to see Me. Then the just and upright will answer Him, Lord, when did we see You hungry and gave You food, or thirsty and gave You something to drink? And when did we see You a stranger and welcomed and entertained You, or naked and clothed You? And when did we see You sick or in prison and came to visit You? And the King will reply to them, Truly I tell you, in so far as you did it for one of the least [in the estimation of men] of these My brethren, you did it for Me."*

In our scribal ministry, we have to be sensitive to the needs of God's people. This passage of scripture in no way indicates that we are to come down to the level of the sinner. It doesn't mean we have to dress like them, talk like them or walk like them. It means that we must MEET THEM in their place of need by the Spirit of the Lord. This is why we can't simply make a decision to recite or read a favorite poem, sing a particular song, conduct a play the way we feel or share a certain short story or inspirational word. We have to allow the Lord to tell us what to share and when! It may seem out of place or inappropriate but God knows all. Truly, this is ministry - meeting people where Jesus would have met them. We have so much light to present to God's people. Our scribal ministry must be so pure that that the words God speak through us will truly draw men unto him.

If you found out that today was your last day on earth, wouldn't you spend it sharing your heart with your loved ones and pressing them not to forget your words? Well, Jesus did that with his disciples. After the crucifixion and resurrection, he appeared one last time to his disciples, and he said to them:

"... All authority (all power of rule) in heaven and on earth has been given to me. Go then and make disciples of all the nations, baptizing (immersing) them into the name of the Father and of the Son and of the Holy Spirit, teaching them to observe everything that I have commanded you, and behold, I am with you all the days (perpetually, uniformly, and on every occasion), to the [very] close and consummation of the age. Amen (so let it be)." **Matthew 28:18-20**

We must use everything that we have been given to fulfill our destiny and purpose in Christ Jesus. Reconciliation is at the very heart of God. It doesn't matter whether God is using us to bring correction and repentance to the church or whether he's using us to invite the sinner in to the brotherhood of believers.

What does matter is that we do all that is required of us concerning *the Kingdom* so that we can stand blameless in the presence of our God. When we fail to walk in our authority and power, many souls are lost. Just as with an army platoon – one soldier out of position – can wreak havoc on the entire camp. There are numerous examples of this in the word. Ezra knew this. He used his scribal ministry to draw men unto God. At every opportunity he preached the word and he purposed in his heart that he would keep its statutes. Do what God has commanded you to do. Many, many souls are depending on you.

Romans 5:19 says, *"For as by one man's disobedience many were made sinners, so also by one man's obedience many will be made righteous."* Disobedience affects everyone. It's not just about what's going to happen to you. It's about what is going to happen to the generations in your lineage and the souls you have been ordained to reach.

A Closer Look at Your Scribal Ministry

"Do not neglect the gift that is in you, which was given to you by prophecy with the laying on of the hands of the eldership." -- *1 Timothy 4:14*

Don't minimize your scribal ministry. You are needed in the body of Christ! It grieves my heart to hear the testimony of believers who sit quietly in church congregations holding back prophetic poems, inspirational writings, prophetic prayers and other creative works because they do not think what they have is important. It grieves me even more to see these gifts minimized by leaders or set aside during times of worship and praise when they should be coming forth. Every single person – and their ministry – is needed in the body. There are many who write the prophetic creative word of the Lord. But they have no direction, no outlet and no one to talk with who seems to understand. More than ever, we must allow the Lord to lead and guide our steps.

It's not unusual for a scribal gift to be seen as insignificant or viewed as a form of entertainment in the body. This happens, for the most part, because people lack the teaching or they just don't understand the purpose for the gift. Even the scribes themselves sometimes see their gifts as entertainment! Every now and then I see scribal ministry come forth in the form of plays or as words of encouragement and hope during funerals, weddings on various holidays – especially Valentine's Day, Easter, Christmas and Mother's Day. I'm not trying to be comical here, but it's the truth. You're not a *holiday* poet. You're not just a playwright whose productions come forth at Easter. You're not a "wedding poet" or "wedding focused inspirational writer." You are a minister of the gospel who uses written words as your sword and shield.

It is through your pen and paper or keyboard and mouse that God will deliver *nations* into your hands for restoration through salvation, deliverance and healing. Our Father in heaven does not want you to limit your potential. There are many prophetic writers who have been folded into theatrical ministries or onto poetry teams where the focus may be on presenting and performing the gift, instead of cultivating it by the Spirit.

Right now, the Lord is saying to you, *"I want to take you higher. It's time to cultivate the Scribal Anointing upon your life and go to new heights and levels in me."* The plans God has for us are free of limits and boundaries in him. No gift is too small for God! I really pray that you get this! Everyone's ministry is significant. I wish I could shout this from the rooftop of every building in the world.

1 Corinthians 12:17-23: *"If the whole body were an eye, where would be the hearing? If the whole were hearing, where would be the smelling? But now God has set the members, each one of them, in the body just as He pleased. And if they were all one member, where would the body be? But now indeed there are many members, yet one body. And the eye cannot say to the hand, "I have no need of you"; nor again the head to the feet, "I have no need of you." No, much rather, those members of the body which seem to be weaker are necessary. And those members of the body which* **we think to be less honorable, on these we bestow greater honor...** *"*

Now look at our Father. In his word, he chooses to exalt those whom others consider to be "less." Nothing is insignificant in the hands of God. We do, however, have to remember this: **Our writings *will never* supersede the word of God, but for someone who may not know him that testimony or prayer you write could be just the link they need to jumpstart their journey in Christ.** Your gift is a vehicle to either plant or water godly seeds in the lives of those who hear or read the prophetic words that flow from your spirit. My walk with God, just like yours, *is not* predicated on the gift – but on our obedience to God.

In his own words Jesus said to Peter, *"If you love me, feed my sheep."* **John 21:16**

To claim our place as "scribes instructed in the Kingdom of Heaven" we are saying that we have committed our whole being to God – spirit, soul and body. It means that our lifestyle is righteous and that our motives for ministering are Christ-like. It means that you are willing to be obedient to what is required of you. Some soul somewhere is waiting on you to walk out your destiny. If I had chosen to ignore the unction to write this book, there's no telling HOW MANY souls would have missed their increase in scribal ministry! Voices of Christ would not exist as a Prophetic School of the Scribe! The increase of this entire ministry was hidden in the writing and releasing of this single book! I pray that you are hearing what Father is saying in the midst of this.

Do you realize that an aspect of your destiny or purpose is hidden in what has been entrusted or released to you? When you fail to follow-through, you DENY yourself and others that place of destiny and purpose in the Lord. Ask yourself this question, *"Why am I in pursing my scribal ministry?"* Then give the Holy Spirit permission to show you the answer.

Scribes of the King, your ministry is not just about YOU! The lives of others are hanging in the balance. Every Holy Spirit inspired work that you publish is an assignment from God. There are people assigned to you right now that *only you* can reach. Have you prepared your heart to give them what God has placed in your hand?

There are three categories of people in this world who claim to love and serve God. They are true believers, carnal and compromising Christians, and those who are angels of darkness parading as light. As you read this section, don't go through it at it as if you're reading about someone else. Take a self-inventory.

1 Samuel 16:7: *"But the LORD said to Samuel, do not look at his appearance or at his physical stature because I have refused him. For the LORD does not see as man sees;* **for man looks at the outward appearance, but the LORD looks at the heart."**

Three Types of Christian Writers

I believe there are three types of Christian writers we encounter in the marketplace ministry and within our congregations. We really can't move any further in expounding upon The Scribal Anointing® without examining this area and bringing understanding. Those three types include:

1) The Christian writer
2) Writers who are Christian
3) Prophetic writers

How do we define the Christian writer? A Christian writer is a true disciple of Christ who has dedicated and committed their lives to writing, recording, documenting or publishing work that exemplify Christ and fortify people in the Word. This group may embrace cessationism, the doctrine that spiritual gifts such as speaking in tongues, prophecy and healing ceased with the original twelve apostles. They also do not believe that there are any more apostles today, only those who existed in biblical times. They do, however, write with the intent of igniting the hearts of men concerning salvation and God's plan for mankind. Writers, however, tend to be very safe and non-revelational in their presentation of the word; and adherence to the foundation of the faith. **Matthew 28:18-20** is lived by this type of writer; however, there is not a deep tapping into for the secret things. They hold strongly to only teaching what is actually literally present in the scripture as it relates to present day.

How do we define writers who are Christian? This category is filled with what we might call religious believers or carnal believers, those who profess faith but have absolutely no evidence of it in their lives outside of a verbal confession. Their scribal projects are rooted in the flesh. There is absolutely no burden for Christ or his message, concern for biblical soundness, living a life that coincides with the scripture or otherwise presenting the Gospel in a way that is glorifying to God exclusively.

This group of believers have great concern for pleasing people, fitting in with others, satisfying fan bases or otherwise relating to the world system. They value publishing and promoting their un-renewed imagination and perspectives while professing their faith, and attending or participating in religious services. Compromise is at the very center of their activities. They tend to greatly hinder the Gospel with extensive perversion and perspectives. **(1 Corinthians 3:1-3)**

How do we define the prophetic writer? A prophetic writer is a true disciple of Christ who has dedicated and committed their lives to writing, recording, documenting or publishing work that exemplify Christ and fortify people in the Word. The difference is that this type of writer has embraced all the gifts of the Holy Spirit in their lives and ministry. They embrace what it means to be prophetic.

Identifying Sheep, Goats & Wolves

If nothing else, a powerful picture has been painted concerning what true scribal ministry looks like among the congregation. In the previous section, we looked at three categories of Christian writers that are among us. Those categories can be instrumental in identifying the spiritual climate surrounding some prophetic writers; and gauging the kinds of scribal projects that are lining summer reading lists at libraries, schools; the shelves of popular book stores; scoring high on the big screen monthly; or meeting us on stage in sold-out theatrical performances all in the name of Christ. In addition to this, however, we have prophetic writers who find themselves in the midst of other "Christian" writers whose motives and intent run deeper than just being carnal or rejecting the work of the Spirit based on theology.

Matthew 25:32-33 says, *"All the nations will be gathered before Him, **and He will separate them one** from another, **as a shepherd divides his sheep from the goats.** And **He will set the sheep on His right hand,** but **the goats on the left."***

Matthew 7:15 says, *"Beware of false prophets, who come to you in sheep's clothing, but **inwardly they are ravenous wolves**."*

Recognizing Sheep

In considering our previous topic, "Three Types of Christian Writers," we can clearly see that sheep would fall into the category of Christian writers and prophetic writers, since both groups have a genuine desire to please and honor God. They love the things God loves and hate the things He hates. They are "salvation focused and Kingdom centered" – committed to presenting the gospel to the very best of their understanding and belief.

Recognizing Goats

Goats, however, fully represent the category of "Writers who are Christian." While they have professed their faith in Christ, they continue to live and exist within the confines of their own mind or understanding. They are still responding to live from their "old nature" – and have not become that new creation. These types of writers, however, tend to like where they are and thrive there. They have grown to love the things of the world and tend to enjoy luring others into "goat status" – eating everything in their path, planting nothing, and then leaving the land devastated before moving on to something else. **(1 John 2:15-16; Revelations 3:15-16; Matthew 6:23-24)**

Recognizing Wolves

Proverbs 26:24-26 says, *"He who hates, disguises it with his lips, And lays up deceit within himself; When he speaks kindly, do not believe him, **For there are seven abominations in his heart; Though his <u>hatred is covered by deceit,</u>** His wickedness will be revealed before the assembly."*

There are many scribes among the congregation who claim to love Christ. At some point, however, we must realize some of the people around us are not "Christians" at all – but people who hate Christ that have infiltrated the congregation for the singular purposes of wreaking havoc among the people. They are not saved – never have been. In addition, they have no intention of coming into the Good Shepherd's fold. These types of scribes are WOLVES. People can and do write and publish books under the label of Christian simply as a marketing or promotional tool. **2 Corinthians 11:14-15** says, *"And no wonder, for Satan himself masquerades as an angel of light. It is not surprising, then, if his servants masquerade as servants of righteousness. Their end will be what their actions deserve."*

*"These people honor me with their lips, **but their hearts are far from me.**" --Matthew 15:8*

We must face the fact that there are writers who claim to be prophetic and who claim Christ that truly have no regard for our Lord, and they are tapping into a prophetic source that is not of our God. They are counterfeits sent to plant seeds of destruction and discord among the people of God. Writers operating in this arena often mix their writing with godly principles, mysticism, self-discovery, inner healing, spiritual enlightenment, and other doctrines that can be difficult to identify. Wisdom, knowledge and understanding in the midst of discernment and intercession are your greatest weapons against this type of deception.

"Watch out for false prophets. They come to you in sheep's clothing, but inwardly they are ferocious wolves." **Matthew 7:15**

PART IV: BREAKING SPIRITUAL STRONGHOLDS

*"Now these are the ones sown among thorns; they are the ones who
hear the word, and the cares of this world, the deceitfulness of riches,
and the desires for other things entering in choke the word, and it becomes unfruitful."*
~ Mark 4:18, 19

MINISTRY VS ENTERTAINMENT

"Many plans are in a man's mind, but it is the Lord's purpose for him that will stand."
~**Proverbs 19:21**

This is not a popular topic. In fact, I can say that I have received some of my greatest criticism in ministry from Christians when addressing it. Why? Well, this particular topic exposes the work of the flesh and confronts the underlining motives that lead believers to pimp and prostitute their gifts and ministry. God has given Voices of Christ a mandate to raise 21st century scribes for pure ministry and part of that training is inscribing this message upon the hearts of men: *"Jesus Christ did not come to entertain you, but to set the captives free!"*

Defining Pure Ministry

I've found that the best approach to this subject is to begin by providing biblical definitions of the words "minister" and "ministry" and then building on this foundation. The word minister is translated as *"diakonos"* in Greek and it is defined as "one who accomplishes and completes the instructions or commands of a master." From this point forward when you see the word minister before a name or if someone says that they are ministering the gospel, they are actually saying, "I am accomplishing or completing the instructions or commands of a master." The question that is at the forefront of my heart, however, is this: Who is your master?

Now, consider the word **ministry**. Its Greek origin is *"leitourgevw"* and it has several related meanings. It means (1) to do a service or to perform the work of priests and Levites who were bruised with sacred rites in the tabernacle of the temple; (2) Christians serving Christ, whether by prayer or instructing others concerning the way of salvation or in some other way; (3) Those who aid others with their resources and relieve their poverty, and (4) To assume an office which must be administered at one's own expense.

Now, when you see or hear the word ministry from this point forward begin to think of it in the context of each one of the biblical definitions above. Consider the ministry of the High Priests in the Old Covenant and the ministry of Jesus Christ in the New Covenant. You will see that both were required to: (1) perform specific tasks for the Kingdom, (2) serve other followers of God concerning the law, (3) aid others in their poverty, and (4) assume offices in which sacrifices were required. Are these four areas evident by demonstration in your ministry?

When we talk about looking to Jesus as our example for ministry, shouldn't our lives reflect the example he left? This is a simple, straight forward question. How many people in your circle of friends are actually seeking to follow the example Christ left? Take a look at this short list of reasons why Jesus came from heaven to earth.

Jesus came from heaven to earth:

- To ransom and purchase salvation for mankind.
- To lead mankind into repentance.
- To be a light to the world.
- To give abundant life.
- To fulfill the law and the prophets.
- To tell the world about the Kingdom of God.
- To demonstrate the love of God.
- To do the will of his Father in heaven.
- To bear witness to the truth.
- To bring division among men.

The reasons why Jesus came clearly show that his purposes on earth were rooted in serving others and pleasing God. This is what pure ministry is all about. Before ascending to heaven for the final time, Jesus left clear instructions to the disciples. In **Matthew 28:18-20** he said: *"…all authority has been given to Me in heaven and on earth. Go therefore and make disciples of all the nations, baptizing them in the name of the Father and of the Son and of the Holy Spirit, teaching them to observe all things that I have commanded you; and lo, I am with you always, even to the end of the age."*

But Jesus did not stop there. He had previously told his disciples that they would do greater works than he did. He said that signs, wonders and miracles would follow them. Every gift, every office and every ministry has been given this charge. We are not just going out making disciples and teaching people the gospel just to do it. God has a purpose and that purpose is to become a bridge of reconciliation for those in sin.

1 Corinthians 5:17-19: *"Therefore if any person is [engrafted] in Christ (the Messiah) he is a new creation (a new creature altogether); the old [previous moral and spiritual condition] has passed away. Behold, the fresh and new has come! But all things are from God, who through Jesus Christ reconciled us to Himself [received us into favor, brought us into harmony with Himself] and **gave to us the ministry of reconciliation** [that by word and deed we might aim to bring others into harmony with Him]. It was God [personally present] in Christ, reconciling and restoring the world to favor with Himself, not counting up and holding against [men] their trespasses [but cancelling them], **and committing to us the message of reconciliation (of the restoration to favor)."***

This is what every disciple of Christ should be doing in the body – no matter the gift. But because you are scribes, you must realize that your gift is simply a tool to assist you in moving forward in ministry. Like a wrench, hammer or screw driver, every tool has a specific operation it must perform – otherwise that tool is useless. We have very clear guidelines on how to use our tools.

2 Timothy 4:1-5 says: *"I charge you in the presence of God and of Jesus Christ, who is the judge of the living and the dead, and by (in light of) His coming and His Kingdom: **Herald and preach the word!***

**Keep your sense of urgency (standby, be at hand and ready), whether the opportunity is favorable or unfavorable,** _whether it is convenient or inconvenient, whether it is welcome or unwelcome. You as a preacher of the word are to show people in the way their lives are wrong. And convince them, rebuking and correcting, warning and encouraging them, being unflagging and inexhaustible in patience and teaching._

"For the time is coming **_when people will not tolerate (endure) sound and wholesome instruction, but having ears itching for something pleasing and gratifying._** _They will gather themselves one teacher after another to a considerable number, chosen to satisfy their own liking and to foster errors they hold, and turn aside from hearing the truth and wonder off into myths and man-made fictions._

"But as for you, be calm and steady, accept and suffer unflinchingly every hardship, do the work of an evangelist, fully perform all the duties of your ministry."

This passage clearly establishes how we are to approach the Gospel. Our instructions are to (1) herald and preach the word, (2) Keep our sense of _urgency_ in favourable and unfavourable conditions, (3) Show people in the ways their lives are wrong and convince them with encouragement, correction and warning to do right, (4) Remain calm and steady, and (5) Accept and endure the hardship that comes with the ministry, (6) Evangelize, and (7) fulfill the duties of your ministry.

I want you to understand that these are the areas of ministry that define our love walk with Christ. If we love him the way we proclaim from our lips, then we will love the people he has sent us to disciple enough to see that that have an opportunity to receive the gospel. It is critical that we submit to this call to ministry. This passage of scripture is a call to ministry. A title, degree or ordination is not a call! A call, by biblical definition, is a call into service.

The only way to understand what entertainment really is means that we have to look at what ministry really is to God. Let's take a closer look at the seven points mentioned above.

1. **Herald and preach the word.** Shout, publish, proclaim, teach and spread the word of God. When we write or speak as a messenger of God, we are saying that, "God told me to tell you these things." Either be prepared to give them what the Lord is really saying – which will line up with the scriptures every time – or be prepared to suffer the consequences of lying on God.

2. **Keep a sense of urgency in favorable and unfavorable conditions.** Time is short. We do not know the day or the hour when Christ will return. We do not know how much time God has allotted us to live. With that in mind, we must live our lives as if this is the very last opportunity we will have on earth to share the good news. This is the urgency our Father speaks of here. It also shouldn't matter to us what others might think of our actions.

After all, it's not about them. It's about fulfilling God's call for every believer. It grieves my spirit to see people attend a Christian "event" and then leave without even getting an opportunity to give or rededicate their lives to Christ.

3. **Show people in the ways their lives are wrong and convince them with encouragement correction and warning to do right.** With a spirit of love, humility and encouragement, we should be showing people through the scriptures how life should be lived. Be patience and help them achieve understanding. All of your writings should fall in one or more of these three categories.

4. **Remain calm and steady.** It can be difficult sometimes to talk about Jesus in a setting that seems to reject him. God wants us to have confidence in him and the ability of the Holy Spirit to guide us in every area of ministry. This calmness is nothing more than faith and confidence in God.

5. **Accept and endure the hardship that comes with the ministry.** Stop complaining. Accept the fact that persecution and struggle comes with walking in a pure ministry. Be worried however, if no persecution comes. This may be a sign that you are on the wrong team.

6. **Evangelize.** Look for an opportunity to share the Gospel wherever you go.

7. **Fulfill the duties of your ministry.** If you are a scribe, then you are obligated to learn about and exercise in all areas of your scribal ministry. Action, when undertaken in the will of God, will always accelerate your destiny and purpose in Christ.

A Close Look at Entertainment

Father, in the name of your son Jesus, I pray now, that as we step into deeper waters in understanding our purpose as present day scribes that the scales placed over our eyes because of sin and ignorance will be lifted. I pray that every mind-blocking spirit that seeks to prevent this message from reaching the hearts of your people be broken, right now, in Jesus name. I pray that you will give them a heart of flesh that they may receive your word, in Jesus name. I pray that they take the road called strait and the path called narrow that has been set before them on this day, in Jesus name. Convict! Deliver! Heal and set free! In Jesus' Name.

In truth, there is absolutely no biblical foundation for entertainment as we know it today in our western culture. The only "Gospel Entertainment Industry" that exists is the one born of this world – out of the flesh and desires of men. Please understand, there is absolutely nothing wrong with publishing the Word of the Lord by any means necessary but this publishing must set the stage for the call to believe – nothing else.

The world has entertainment but the Kingdom has fellowship. All through the scriptures, the celebrations and festivals that went forth that were OF GOD – commemorated a move of God or existed in the confines of the "brotherhood." Our celebrations and festivals were NEVER for the idolaters or unbelievers. Our coming together, as one in Christ, has always been intended for intimacy before the Lord. When the consecrated gift goes forth, it goes forth in the midst of a consecrated people. Generally speaking, anyone who was not a part of that would either be transformed in Father's presence or separated by His judgment.

Father has not changed. There will be people OUTRAGED by this entire teaching, but I tell you, I wish we would be outraged by the rape of the Word; the twisting of scripture to fit the culture of this generation; and the hatred for the congregation! What if we worshipped Christ like we worship at football games and concerts! What if we could turn that seemingly acceptable response to superstars to intercession and prayer!

In the King James Bible **entertain** is only mentioned once and that reference is in **Hebrews 13:1-2:** *"Let brotherly love continue. Do not forget to **entertain** strangers, for by so doing some have unwittingly **entertained** angels."*

The Greek origin of the word entertain is "xenizo." It means to be received as a guest and to extend hospitality or kindness to someone. In the Greek Translation of the Bible, this is what this passage of scripture was referring to. There is no word for "entertain" in Hebrew as we understand it today or use it in the midst of our congregations. The closest meaning is the word "invite" and it is used in the sense of inviting someone to a marriage feast. The culture of Moses and the culture of Christ is one deeply rooted in family and hospitality. Their traditions as revealed in the scriptures, commentaries, articles and personal testimonies further reveal this. In your own studies, you will find that this makes a whole lot more sense in the spirit and in the natural verses what we see in the western Church today.

In Jewish culture, the word hospitality means to provide provision for as in food, water, shelter and protection to travellers, guests or others in need. Sometimes that provision extended itself to sending an escort to accompany the stranger, traveller or guest as they moved to the next phase of their journey. This wasn't a burden, but a common and expected practice that showed respect, concern, kindness and honor for the well-being of another. Without this type of concern, a traveller could be robbed, maimed or even killed along their journey. The parable of the Samaritan, in its simplest form, really highlights the meaning of "entertain" as Father intended.

This is what entertaining means in the scriptures! Today, it is looked upon as amusement, recreation, pleasure or a *diversion* presented by a performer and designed to hold the attention of an audience or its participants. It promotes self-gratification and idol worship. Entertainment executed in this manner is the way of the world – not the way of God. Clearly you can see that the biblical basis for entertainment and the worldly basis of entertainment conflict greatly.

This doesn't mean that God does not want you to enjoy life. It doesn't mean that Christians cannot get together to share their scribal gifts and talents or other sacred arts. When we gather together in this way, it is PRAISE & WORSHIP. This is what God has given the body! Our gathers are those that exalt Him and prepare a place for His dwelling. Father NEVER gave the body of Christ an "entertainment" mentality.

Well, the bible tells us that the joy of the Lord is our strength. It also tells us that laughter is like medicine to the soul. There is not a single scripture in the bible that tells us we must be "stiff-necked and religious." But we must be watchful in presenting everything we do unto God as A SACRIFICE of worship and praise. He is a HOLY GOD! Check out the chart on the next page that distinguishes between "a minister and an entertainer" as we discuss it here.

Let's look at the biblical differences of a minister of the gospel verses an entertainer:

A Minister Is:	An Entertainer Is:
God focused	Self-focused
Excited about spreading God's word	Excited about spreading one's product or service
Unwilling to compromise	Willing to compromise
Focused on teaching and demonstrating the word of God	Focused on performance, pleasing man and amusement
Willing to sacrifice self to please God	Not willing to give up personal needs or wants
Using his/her gifts to draw men to God	Using his/her gifts for profit or personal gain
Committed to pushing people toward God	Committed to drawing people to self
Led by the Holy Spirit	Led by the crowd
Draws strength from the company of believers	Mixes company with believers and world
Set apart and separated from the world	Difficult to distinguish from the world
Willing to sacrifice all for Jesus Christ	Will stand for what is politically correct or what feels right
Driven by an urgency to share the gospel	Driven by an urgency to be seen , heard and successful
Has a heart for winning souls	Have a heart for money, success and power
**Continue adding to this list as the Holy Spirit reveals areas of instability and compromise to you.	

2 Corinthians 6:14: *"…Do not be yoked with unbelievers. For what do the righteousness and wickedness have in common? Or what fellowship can light have with darkness? What harmony is there between Christ and Belial? What does a believer have in common with an unbeliever? What agreement is there between the temple of God and idols?* **For we are the temple of the living God.** *As God has said, I will live in them* *and walk among them, and I will be their God and they will be my people. Therefore, come out from among them and be separate, says the Lord."*

I have met many ministers and worship arts leaders over the years who love God. Sadly, they were trained under "Christians" whose perception of ministry was based on ungodly practices. As a result, they have spent their lives imitating and practicing what they have been taught. Are they to blame? No, not completely. They are, however, responsible once they receive the truth.

On the same note, I've met those who do know better. But because their focus is on drawing people to their church, organization, to them or event – they feel that they are justified in doing whatever it takes to reach the people. Father doesn't want US putting OUR HANDS on HIS PEOPLE. We have to do what HE requires! Let him teach you what is pleasing to him by spending more time in study and prayer.

The Effects of Walking in a Spirit of Entertainment

"Adulterers and adulteresses! **Do you not know that friendship with the world is enmity with God? Whoever therefore wants to be a friend of the world makes himself and enemy with God.** *Or do you think the scriptures say in vain, The Spirit who dwells within us yearns jealousy? God resists the proud, but gives grace to the humble.*

Therefore, submit to God. Resist the devil and he will flee from you. Draw near to God and he will draw near to you. Cleans your hands, you sinners; and purify your hearts, you double-minded. Lament and mourn and weep! Let your laughter be turned to mourning and your joy to gloom. Humble yourselves in the sight of the Lord and he will lift you up." **James 4:4-7**

There are many who think God is blessing "entertainment." God cannot bless something that he did not create. God cannot bless a system that is rooted in sin and contradicts his word. Our Father is NOT the God of entertainment.

Luke 16:15 says, *"...you are the ones who justify yourselves in the eyes of men, but God knows your hearts.* **What is highly valued among men is detestable in God's sight.***"*

What do you value?

This spirit of entertainment has infiltrated the body of Christ and raped the ministry of praise and worship of its anointing and power. The very gifts that were intended to exalt God and encourage his children in the ministry are now no different from television or radio pop culture. Many try to say that the times have changed, when the truth of the matter is that men have changed gods.

God is not the author of the "entertainment" industry, gospel showdowns and talent searches, literary competitions and contests. God did not create some of this music we listen to on the airways and claim as praise and worship. Many of these songs and music competitions are birth from the soulish realm, and some are demonic in nature. The vast majority, however, lean toward the soul. A key indicator is this: *Would God take something that satan created, change the words around a little to sound holy, and then sign his name on it? Would God line up all the poets in heaven and have a poetry slam and then choose the best poem from among the contestants? Would God host a gospel music showcase and award a prize to the best musician?* These are legitimate questions. I encourage you to present them to the Holy Spirit, and patiently await his answer. I am convinced that Heaven releases an authentic sound! I am convinced that Heaven has its own culture.

Let's look at entertainment first.

Fact: Entertainment pleases the flesh. A person who entertains is constantly being placed in position to create a better show every time they go before people. With each performance, the pressure to please the people in attendance increase. The need to stay ahead of what other entertainers are doing increases. The focus is solely on presenting the best show so that the people will want more of that person, the idea or the ideals that they are presenting.

Pure ministry feeds the spirit while purging the soul of sin and realigning the will of men with the mind of Christ. What comes forth during ministry is under the complete control of the Holy Spirit. So because of that, it is up to the Holy Spirit to meet the needs of those who are benefiting from the ministry. The minister, in essence, is simply a vessel used by God.

Ecclesiastes 3:16 says, *"I know that whatever God does, It shall be forever. Nothing can be added to it, And nothing taken from it. God does it that men should fear before Him."*

When we walk under a cloud of entertainment, we open the door to a spirits of competition, comparison and compromise.

There are also many believers who hold contests, gospel showdowns, showcases, talent searches and other competitions in the name of Jesus. The popular thinking here is that it presents an opportunity for believers to raise money and highlight the most talented believers in the process.

The problem is that this is the way the world is set up, not the Kingdom of God.

God would never put his children in direct competition with one another and then select one spiritual gift or talent over the other, and award that spiritual gift with a prize. Clearly, this does not mean that everyone who participates in these activities is hell bound. It does mean that there is a need for biblically sound teaching so that understanding can come and deception can be averted. Many believers simply lack understanding and cannot see the ploy of the enemy.

When we showcase our spiritual gifts and talents or place gifting in competitive formats – we are taking the focus off God and placing it on people. We are giving people "credit" for the abilities or skills they seem possess. We are saying that we "own" the gifts or abilities and have complete control over them. Truly, God receives nothing from this perception or wrong attitude.

Who gave us the right to judge or showcase God's gifts? Competition opens the door for division in the body. It is a breeding ground for pride, jealousy, envy, spite, intimidation, rejection, condemnation, and more. You see, while entertainment opens the door; competition brings division and gives birth to COMPARISON.

So now, you're not only dealing with the sin of entertainment; but have caused the people of God to compete against one another to see who is the best; and then seeds have been planted to cause people to compare "what they've received from God" with what "someone else has received from God." When in truth, there is no comparison. But the role of the enemy here is simply to divide and conquer.

Check out this example. I'm going to release this example in bullet points, so consider each one by the Spirit – not with your mind.

Here we go:

- The gifts inside you belong God.
- The gifts inside me belong God.
- My gift is a facet of God's power, not my own power.
- Your gift is a facet of God's power, not your own power.
- You do not own your gift, but are only a steward of it.
- I do not own my gift. I am just a steward of it.
- When you go forth in your gift, you are doing so in the strength the Lord provides.
- When I go forth in my gift, I do so in the strength the Lord provides.
- You become one with Christ from the minute you entered the Kingdom.
- I became one with Christ from the minute I entered the Kingdom.
- Christ is one with God.
- We are one with God.

My question to you is this: *"If my gift is from God and is released out of His anointing; and your gift is from God and is released out of His anointing. If we are all one with God and God with us, then why would the Lord turn around and compete against Himself? Why would He compare himself to himself?"*

My left arm does not compete with the right, nor the right with the left. **(1 Corinthians 12)**

2 Corinthians 10:12 says this, *"Not that we [have the audacity to] venture to class or [even to] compare ourselves with some who exalt and furnish testimonials for themselves! However, **when they measure themselves with themselves and compare themselves with one another**, they are without understanding and behave unwisely."*

Entertainment is a powerful satanic weapon that has been unleashed in the body. If not recognized, it will burn like wildfire in the hearts of men – feeding on the darkness in their hearts. Our Father's desire is to see each one of us work in harmony with one another – not exalting and worshiping the gift. The scriptures tell us that we have one body but many members. All the members work together for the benefit of all. With this in mind, it should be evident that the "superiority" of one gift is completely irrelevant. God has no respecter of persons.

Also consider this.

As a result of comparison and competition in the world and in the body, we have many children, youth, teens and young adults who are aspiring to be like someone else instead of seeking their own unique savour and identity in Christ. Subtly, the spirit of entertainment is giving birth to idol worship as well as the desire to be worshiped. God wants *his word (Jesus Christ)* to have the greatest impact and effect on our lives. Whether we like it or not, we have already chosen a master. Not everyone may be able to recognize that they have made a choice, but believe me when I say: A choice has already been made.

The heart of every ministry should be rooted in seeing "soul transformation in Christ." Jesus came to set the captives free. **Luke 4:17-19** says:

"And He was handed the book of the prophet Isaiah. And when He had opened the book, He found the place where it was written:

The Spirit of the LORD is upon Me,
*Because He has **anointed Me***
***To preach the gospel** to the poor;*
*He has sent Me **to heal the broken hearted,***
To proclaim liberty to the captives
*And **recovery of sight to the blind,***
To set at liberty those who are oppressed;
***To proclaim the acceptable year** of the LORD."*

This strong stand in the word does not mean that God will not send some people into places where entertainment is going forth. In fact, many will be walking into these arenas. We have to remember that wherever there is darkness, there must be light. Just as satan has wolves in sheep's clothing lurking about in the earth, God has watchman and intercessors of light standing in the midst of darkness as well. The key here is this: You must be a light.

On the flip-side, I've bumped into many carnal Christians who write worldly material and then try to give God credit for it. I firmly believe credit goes to their own soul! I went to an open mic one night and heard a poem written by a skilled and popular poet here in the Atlanta area. It had curse words and all manner of raunchiness in it. Some months later, I saw him again at a Christian open mic where we were both presenting. He used the same poem, but changed the wording around to fit "the climate" so to speak. My spirit was grieved! How easy it was for Him to exchange wedding rings before a Holy God! God received no glory from this, and in truth, those listening received a corrupted word… a message from a forked tongue.

You see, compromising Christians know the truth but they choose to walk on a path that is pleasing to man, to self. If you are walking with someone who does this, yet claim they love God bring them into the knowledge of the truth. If they refuse to hear the truth, it's time to separate from them. You don't have to go pray about it. You can walk away right them, and then go pray "for" them. If you are this person, "Repent!"

2 Thessalonians 3:6, *"But we command you, brethren, in the name of our Lord Jesus Christ, that you withdraw from every brother who walks **disorderly** and not according to the tradition which he received from us."*

Motives & Motivation

"A good man out of the good treasure of his heart brings forth good things, and an evil man out of the evil treasure brings forth evil things." --**Matthew 12:35**

The word motive is simple to define. It refers to the reasons behind our actions. When scripture speaks of motives, it delves into the true, hidden intent of the heart. This is important because when God searches for his children, he is searching for the motives behind the action or lack of.

"I know, my God, that you test the heart and have pleasure in uprightness. As for me, in the uprightness of my heart …" --**1 Chronicles 29:17**

"The spirit of a man is the lamp of the Lord, Searching all the inner depths of his heart." --**Proverbs 20:27**

"I, the Lord, search the heart, I test the mind, even to give every man according to his ways, According to the fruit of his doings." --**Jeremiah 17:10**

So many people use the gifts of God for personal gain.

I ask you today: "Why do you write, preach or prophesy? Why did you publish your book or CD? Why do you attend open mics or poetry readings? Why do you share your poetry with others?" Well, motives are important to God. Outward appearances and good intentions can be very deceptive.

There are many dreams that I've held in my heart since childhood concerning things I've wanted to do. For the longest time, I thought it was okay to have these dreams and desires until one day, I heard a preacher say: "We must learn to commit our hopes and dreams to the Lord. Some of us are praying for things and asking for things that are not a part of God's will for our lives. We are seeking things that are not God's design for us. We must stop, and ask him what it is that he wants for us and then allow him turn our hearts toward those things."

I was immediately convicted. Many of my dreams came from television influences, books that I read or things that I may have seen others doing that brought them reverence, respect popularity and honour. On top of that, all I could think of was how people always said "that girl ain't going to amount to anything." So in my mind, I wanted to do something BIG… something that would prove to others that I was "worth something" or to prove that they were wrong. I had an "I'll show you" attitude for just about everything. I thank God that I purged my spirit of that stronghold.

My motives were all mixed up – even after I came to the Lord. These aspirations weren't bad; but my reasons for achieving them were. When God asked me why I wanted to write this book, I said to him: "Father, your scribes need to have an identity rooted in you. I want to share what you have given me with them so they can consecrate their ministry back to you, take the world's hands off their gifts and be who you've called them to be in the earth."

The word "motive" simply refers to the meaning behind why a person does something.

Our carnal nature instinctively wants to exalt self. But as the Apostle Paul said we must seek the face of God and die daily to the flesh – confessing our sins and renewing our mind with his word. As scribes, we are constantly fighting that prideful pharisaic spirit and all of its associated demons. To break this stronghold, we must become transparent before God and uncover those little selfish secrets, and then go back to him and say: "Lord, it's not my will but your will be done. Give me the plans and strategies that you have for me Father."

John 4:24-25 says: *"But an hour is coming and now is when the true worshippers shall worship the Father in Spirit and In Truth (not flesh) and truth (unadulterated worship); for such people the Father seeks to be His worshippers. God is a spirit and those who worship him must worship him in Spirit and Truth."*

When my motives were out of place, I was out of the will of God. I had one vision and direction that I wanted to move toward, and God had something completely different. I enjoyed making my way across the open mic scene and performing poetry. But one day, when I was really enjoying myself, he spoke softly into my spirit: *"Theresa, your path is different. Either follow the path I have set for you or I will shut it down."*

I only had to hear this once. I separated myself and set out on the path God had for me. This didn't mean that those around me were necessarily on the wrong path. For all I know, that could be the path God has for them. It just meant that I was out of place and needed to get my heart right. Are you on the path God set for you? Or are you walking down some path that belongs to someone else? In **Jeremiah 28,** the people of God had been given some directives SPECIFIC for them to follow. Afterward, the Lord told them this in **Jeremiah 29:11**.

"For I know the thoughts that I think toward you, says the LORD, thoughts of peace and not of evil, to give you a future and a hope. Then you will call upon Me and go and pray to Me, and I will listen to you. And you will seek Me and find Me, when you search for Me with all your heart. **I will be found by you, says the LORD, and I will bring you back from your captivity; I will gather you from all the nations and from all the places where I have driven you, says the LORD, and I will bring you to the place from which I cause you to be carried away captive."**

If you are on the wrong path, God is ready and willing to turn it around right now. All He needs is a sincere heart.

Simply:
1. **Trust God. Believe him.** First, you must trust and believe that God's plans for your life are better than the ones you have. Lay your plans down! Give them up! Seek God's will for your life. Desire to put on the mind of Christ daily.

2. **Allow Holy Spirit to give you a heart for prayer.** You've got to have a prayer life. He has promised that if you come to him he will listen.

3. **Seek Him, long for His presence.** In your prayer time you must seek him with all you heart for divine direction and answers to anything that concerns you. He's looking for your willingness and desire to obey him.

If you believe his word and do this, he promises that he will bring you out of your captivity and return you to the place you were BEFORE you chose the wrong path. Restoration and right standing is just a prayer away. I hear this in my spirit right now. If you believe the word of the prophet, God is going to turn things around for you right now. Our motives MUST be pure – or they will lead us down a path of destruction.

"Beloved, I pray that you may prosper in all things and be in health, just as your soul prospers."
3 John 1:2

PART V: UNLEASHING THE SCRIBAL ANOINTING

"And when they had laid many stripes on them, they threw them into prison, commanding the jailer to keep them securely. Having received such a charge, he put them into the inner prison and fastened their feet in the stocks. But at midnight Paul and Silas were praying and singing hymns to God, and the prisoners were listening to them. Suddenly there was a great earthquake, so that the foundations of the prison were shaken; and immediately all the doors were opened and everyone's chains were loosed."
~Acts 16:23-26

WHEN BREAKTHROUGH DOESN'T COME

The greatest hindrance to truth in the body of Christ is **ignorance.** The deeper we go into a place of ignorance concerning the things of God, the closer we reach a destructive destination.

Hebrews 4:6 says, *"My people are destroyed for **lack of knowledge; because you [the priestly nation] have <u>rejected</u> knowledge,** I will also reject you that **you shall be no priest to Me;** seeing <u>you have forgotten the law of your God,</u> I will also forget your children."*

This is a powerful scripture. It speaks to the very heart of the power of ignorance over the life of a believer. In the context of discussing The Scribal Anointing®, it should be evident that the reason many scribes are self-serving and following the path of "entertainment" verses ministry is because they do not know who they are in Christ. No one has really held us accountable up until now for the full understanding of who we've been called to be.

The Scribal Anointing changes this! NOW- in this moment – you have your true identity if you have completed this book. **Listen, the greatest ministry we can attain to is NOT in the earth – it is in the spirit UNTO GOD. When our hearts come to understand this, we will NEVER despise warnings against serving self and pursuing a life of idolatry. PERIOD.**

It really is that simple. We have been called to be led of the Spirit. As a result of this truth, I am convinced that there are levels of breakthrough that we cannot obtain without overcoming IGNORANCE.

Ephesians 4:17-18 says, *"This I say therefore, and testify in the Lord, that ye henceforth walk not as other Gentiles walk, in the vanity of their mind, **Having the understanding darkened, being alienated from the life of God** <u>through the ignorance that is in them, because of the blindness of their heart...</u>"*

It's as if we are blinded to our true condition. In this discussion, I am defining breakthrough as the process in which we "penetrate or break through" the enemy's defenses, demolish the enemies camp and come through victorious.

I tell you, if you take what Father has released through the pages of this book seriously and allow Holy Spirit to apply those areas that are needed to your life – you will surely reach a place of breakthrough! Breakthrough isn't always about getting over "writer's block" or getting to a place in which you can hear more music, get more poetry or get into the flow of writing that novel. People of God, those are surface things. True breakthrough – busts THROUGH the obstacles that lie at the root of these things. Ignorance is a STRONGHOLD. A stronghold, as we discuss them here, is defined as a fortress that exists around us that the "hardened heart" builds in its rebellion and self-righteousness. This foundation and walls of this fortress are constructed on ungodly thought patterns; vain imaginations; ungodly belief systems; generational curses; mindsets or attitudes; and the outworking of sin that block our ability to properly relate to or build a relationship with God.

A person can be bound by strongholds and not even know it! There may have been many things between the pages of this book that opened your eyes to the true condition of your soul. There are also strongholds that we are well aware of that are operating in our lives – entertainment is one of them. Why? Because it blocks the move of Holy Spirit in your life and in the lives of others – preventing us from seeing ministry or walking in ministry according to the will of God. Strongholds become like fortified cities that have been constructed in such a way that they must be dismantled.

Ephesians 6:12 says, *"For **we wrestle not against flesh and blood,** but against principalities, against powers, against the rulers of the darkness of this world, against spiritual wickedness in high places."*
2 Corinthians 10:3-5 says, *"For though we walk in the flesh, we do not war after the flesh: (**For the weapons of our warfare are not carnal, but mighty through God to the pulling down of <u>strong holds;</u>**) Casting down imaginations, and <u>**every high thing that exalteth itself against the knowledge of God, and bringing into captivity every thought to the obedience of Christ."**</u>*

God has no problem destroying fortified cities! There are many examples of him doing this in the natural and in the spirit throughout the Old and New Covenants. The Lord has no problem instructing US to destroy fortified cities – which he does consistently in the scriptures. This entire book is written to destroy MANY types of fortified cities in the lives of those who read it.

You see, this teaching is PULLING DOWN strongholds by presenting, teaching and reiterating Father's truth. The words on these pages will bring breakthrough!

The Lord wants to DESTROY your ungodly strongholds. He wants to tear down those walls in your life that prevent you from fulfilling your destiny and purpose in Him. He wants to penetrate the stronghold, get on the inside of each one of us and dismantle them from the inside out! People of God, you must give Holy Spirit your will in order for this to happen.

Again, strongholds have many forms. Some of them are generational and we have no idea they are operating in our lives; and others are obvious.

More than a year ago, I saw a fertile earth in a vision. When I looked to the ground the earth was moist and dark. There were spots and pockets beneath the surface that spelled out the word selfishness. Out of the ground grew a tree whose roots were stamped with the word pride. The tree had a wide trunk and its branches expanded several feet across a blue sky line. From a distance, the tree seemed prosperous, but the closer I walked up to it the branches looked as if they were near death. Each branch had the names of one of the seven things that God hates from **Proverbs 6:16-19** written on the limbs.

They read: a proud look; a lying tongue; hands that shed innocent blood; a heart that devises wicked plans; feet that are swift in running to evil; a false witness who speaks lies, and one who sows discord among brethren.

The tree also had leaves and fruit. But the leaves were sick, and the fruit had stunted growth and resembled crab apples. The fruit had all manner of sins written on them. I knew immediately that they were the offspring of selfishness and pride and other the fruit of the flesh **(Galatians 5:19-21)** were its offspring.

Some biblical characteristics of selfishness are: (1) Pleasing self; (2) Seeking your own profit; (3) Seeking personal gain; (4) Neglecting the needs of others; (5) Performing good deeds for rewards or recognition; and (6) Seeking favor for selfish reasons.

Some biblical characteristics of pride are: (1) Self-Justification; (2) Conceit; (3) Consistently drawing attention to oneself; (4) Self Exaltation; (5) Strong sense of independence or self-sufficiency, and (5) Intense self-admiration that leads to bragging and boasting.

I am convinced that the Lord was showing me strongholds that rest inside of many of those called to scribal ministry. (Please know that there are other types of strongholds like fear, procrastination, etc.; however, I really believe that these are the ones Father wants to deal with most in us.) Take another look at **Matthew 23.**

We are yet in a war – a war for our souls; the souls of others and our very purpose and destiny. People of God, we need breakthrough! Truly, it is time to awaken from our slumber and walk out our purpose and destiny in the Lord.

A Foundation of Prayer

*"All of **you must** keep awake (give strict attention, be cautious and active) **and watch and pray, that you may not come into temptation**. The spirit indeed is willing, but the flesh is weak."*
--**Matthew 26:41**

Obtaining breakthrough begins with prayer.

No matter what we might try to do or say, this simple truth will never, ever change. This place of "keeping awake" as mentioned in the scripture above, is a position of awareness – remaining mindful that the adversary wants to ensnare us and block the Lord's will from coming to past in our lives. So this state of "watching" is actually a place of being vigilant and paying attention to what's going on in our relationship with the Lord. This place of "praying" is a position in Father in which we are seeking, searching, asking and listening for His guidance and directives.

The scripture then says, "that you may not come into temptation." This indicates that "watching and praying" provides some kind of supernatural protection from the adversary. This is POWERFUL! You see, without inviting and evoking the presence of the Lord within us consistently we would not be able to obtain BREAKTHROUGH because the "flesh" – the carnal man – has no TRUE strength without God!

Prayer is at the very foundation of being "kept" out of the way of sin. It is THE ROOT of our strength in the Lord. The bible teaches us clearly that:

- Prayer awakens and charges the spirit;
- Prayer is a place of conception and birth;
- Prayer is a place of growth and maturity;
- Prayer brings the spirit and soul into alignment with the heavenly realm;
- Prayer increases our discernment and causes us to be cautious;
- Prayer increases a deeper longing for intercession;
- Prayer trains our ears to recognize the voice of the Lord;
- Prayer trains our ears to distinguish the Lord's voice from that of a stranger;
- Prayer enables us to speak directly to the Lord;
- Prayer is a place of teaching and training that is intimate between you and the Lord;
- Prayer is a place of protection and the revealing of strategy;
- Prayer is a place of rest;
- Prayer is a place of strategy for intercession;
- Prayer is a place for stirring praise and worship;
- Prayer is a place of seeking and knocking;
- Prayer strengthens and increases trust in the Lord;
- Prayer fine tunes our hearing;
- Prayer increases our belief;
- Prayer opens the door to the spirit realm;
- Prayer open our spiritual eyes and ears;
- Prayer is a place of unlocking secrets and mysteries of the Kingdom; and
- Prayer is place of answers.
- Prayer is a place of intimacy!
- Prayer is a place of revelation, knowledge and understanding!
- Prayer is a place of transformation….

I am not talking about any kind of prayer. I am specifically talking about prayers prayed by those who KNOW Christ and who pray in His name. I can tell you personally that all these things about prayer listed above and more are true.

There are examples all through the word that will support the POWER that is hidden in the kind of prayer spoken of in the word. Personally, I didn't always like prayer or want to pray. A woman of wisdom told me that if *I ever planned* to walk in destiny and purpose that it was the **ONLY** road that could take me there. Today, I've come to give you this exact counsel. I learned quickly that I had to MAKE MYSELF do the very thing that I didn't want to do. In the midst of it, I prayed a simple prayer:

"Holy Spirit give me a love for prayer; and help me develop a heart for prayer and intercession."

I tell you, I asked Father for this and He gave it to me. I still had to do my part. I couldn't wait for the desire to just drop out the sky and for the unction to rise. In my situation, I had to activate that word of prayer by going forth in it.

My prayer was answered. I promise you, people of God, was it not for my prayer life – we would not be discussing *The Scribal Anointing* today. Without prayer, there is no true ministry – just a shell of what could be. Your ministry would end up being a good idea. Without prayer, we cannot clearly hear God or truly embrace any real form of progression.

I had to learn this the HARD way. As a result, I missed some critical moments of destiny in my life that I haven't been able to get back. Not everything can be restored or redeemed to its fullness. **Sampson's life is a perfect example of this.** Read the book of Judges and learn how this anointed, appointed and chosen man of God lost his ministry and ultimately his life. If you have a writer's group, know that the group is first and foremost a prayer team. If you have a weekly open mic, know that first and foremost that open mic must be drenched in prayer. If you have a book or CD project you're working on, know that first and foremost those projects must be cemented in prayer.

Matthew 21:13 says, *"And said unto them*, **It is written**, <u>**My house**</u> **shall be called the house of prayer;** *but ye have made it a den of thieves."*

Unleashing *The Scribal Anointing*® is not about sharing your gift. We must understand that we can do more IN INTERCESSION than we ever could on a stage or behind the pages of a book. In truth, the book is INEFFECTIVE if the vessel being poured into discounts the power of prayer and intercession.

The ministry of prayer is under used and unappreciated by so many of God's people. All of us need to become prayer warriors and intercessors (praying on behalf of others). If ever there was a secret to success – this is it. I firmly believe that if the people of God really gave themselves over to Holy Spirit directed prayer we wouldn't see so much entertainment and false ministry going forth from their ministries in the earth.

Proverbs 19:21 says it this way, *"Many plans are in a man's heart*, **But the counsel of the LORD** *will stand."*

You see, when I was in the world I counted on my "good ideas" getting me what I needed, solving my problems or helping me. In the Kingdom of Heaven, good ideas are irrelevant if they are not born of water and spirit.

Good ideas seem harmless, but I tell you, they are devastating when they are not the "ideas" that Father has set in motion for your destiny. Instead, it can become a hindrance or even a destroyer. There was a man I met once who wanted me to join up with their "gospel street teams" to promote evangelism through the arts. I wanted to be a part of this, but when I went into prayer the Lord said to me plainly, "This is not the path that you are on. Close the door."

For ME, this wasn't God's will even though the benefits of joining were very appealing. This may have been fine for some people, but for me and Voices of Christ it just wasn't God's will! I could only imagine where the ministry would be right now if I had not gone to the Lord in prayer.

This subject is very dear to my heart Scribes of the King. I can't say this enough: "Without prayer there is NO TRUE OR PURE MINISTRY. Without prayer there can be no BREAKTHROUGH OR UNLEASHING OF GODLY PURPOSE."

Who better to navigate our lives than the one who sent our souls from Heaven to earth and has numbered ALL of our days? Who better to tell us when to go and when to stand still than the one who KNOWS the thoughts and the plans He has for us? Sadly, we know this with our lips, but our hearts seem to have difficult time catching up to the revelation here. If you have ever been serious about your life, calling and ministry; then a posture of prayer is your foundational position.

Yeah, I know this wasn't an easy word for some; but what FATHER HAS for you is far greater than anything we could ever think or imagine for ourselves. **Without prayer, neither you nor I will ever truly tap into** *The Scribal Anointing*® **in our lives to the depths Father desires!**

Unveiling the Power of Praise & Worship

Prayer and intercession fuel a desire on the inside of us to praise and worship God. Authentic praise and worship keeps a man's heart broken in the presence of the Lord – even thankful and grateful for the grace and mercy that has been extended to us.

There is courage and a strength that is unleashed in the midst of them that propels us into greatest and literary GIVES BIRTH to purpose. I firmly believe that outside of prayer, this is the next key component to breaking spiritual strongholds.

You see, scriptural examples and personal experiences in my life have shown me that:

- An unclean heart cannot stand in the midst of true praise and worship;
- Heaviness and sorry cannot live in the midst of true praise and worship;
- The lies of the enemy cannot occupy a mind that is drenched in personal praise and worship;
- The spirit of fear can't stand in the midst of exuberant praise and worship;

I could go on and on! There's something about praise and worship that gives the prophetic person a "spiritual enema." It opens up the blocked places, crushes the harden heart or otherwise prepare us for the living water of the spirit to flow.

Praise and worship are states of being – not what you listen to or what you do.

Our daily lives should reflect the very definition of praise which is to release an exuberant offering of gratefulness, reverence and thanksgiving to God that reflects our homage to his majesty, power and love for us – even in silence. Scripture does show us, however, that praise is can be an outward, public and corporate expression of our admiration and reverence to our Father. But I tell you, it is a condition of the heart.

An excellent example of praise can be found in **Psalm 150**. It reads, *"PRAISE THE Lord!* **Praise God in His sanctuary; praise Him in the heavens of His power!** *Praise Him for His mighty acts; praise Him according to the abundance of His greatness! Praise Him with trumpet sound; praise Him with lute and harp! Praise Him with tambourine and [single or group] dance; praise Him with stringed and wind instruments or flutes! Praise Him with resounding cymbals; praise Him with loud clashing cymbals! Let everything that has breath and every breath of life praise the Lord! Praise the Lord! (Hallelujah!)"*

Our daily lives should also release the worship that intensely personal expression of devotion, commitment and faithfulness to God – even in silence. Worship is our way of intimately entering into His presence and allowing Him to fuse our commitment to him in the spirit in every possible way. When I worship, I often feel as if I've entered into a place of death to Theresa and life in Christ. It is a personal and private offering of intimacy, love and adoration; and involves no outside influences. Worship is literally a personal experience between you and Father. When we begin to practice Father's presence through worship, our will is minimized and Father's will over us is exalted… until little by little it takes over places on the inside of us that were previously closed off or inaccessible.

An excellent example of worship can be found in **Revelations 4:8-7** which reads: *"And the four living creatures, individually having six wings, were full of eyes all over and within [underneath their wings];* **and day and night they never stop saying,** *Holy, holy, holy is the Lord God Almighty* **(Omnipotent), Who was and Who is and Who is to come.** *And whenever the living creatures offer glory and honor and thanksgiving to Him Who sits on the throne, Who lives forever and ever (through the eternities of the eternities), The twenty-four elders* **(the members of the heavenly Sanhedrin) fall prostrate before Him Who is sitting on the throne, and they worship Him Who lives forever and ever; and they throw down their crowns before the throne, crying out, Worthy are You, our Lord and God, to receive the glory and the honor and dominion,** *for You created all things; by Your will they were [brought into being] and were created."*

People of God, if you have never experienced true praise or worship – call on Holy Spirit for help. No man can truly take you into those places like God can. Your praise and worship experience should never be dependent solely on music, dance or song. Just thinking about who the Lord is in your life should pull this out of you. This is the place we want to reach.

Other examples of worship are:

- *"Then Abram fell on his face, and God talked with him, saying…"* **–Genesis 17:3** Abram laid before the Lord and worshipped him. In the midst of the worship, God began speaking to Abraham concerning his destiny.

- *"And Joshua fell on his face to the earth and worshiped, and said to Him, "What does my Lord say to His servant?"* –**Joshua 5:15** When Joshua fell on his face to worship the Lord he asked him a question about his destiny and God answered.

- *"And Jehoshaphat bowed his head with his face to the ground, and all Judah and the inhabitants of Jerusalem   bowed   before   the   LORD,   worshiping   the   LORD."* --**2 Chronicles 20:18** When they worshipped the Lord, he gave them a prophetic word concerning divine intervention.

- *"At the evening sacrifice I arose from my fasting; and having torn my garment and my robe, I fell on my knees and spread out my hands to the LORD my God. And I said: "O my God, I am too ashamed and humiliated to lift up my face to You, my God; for our iniquities have risen higher than our heads, and our guilt has grown up to the heavens."* --- **Ezra 9:5**

When worship goes forth, God often shows mercy. Praise and Worship are also weapons of war that assist you in casting down every high thing that exalts itself above God. At one time, I was taught that praise was a weapon of war, but in this walk, I've learned that they both have delivering POWER when you are in the midst of a battle! Those who build strong prayer lives will be led into praise and worship by the Lord; and those who are praise and worshipers will find themselves being drawn into prayer intercession.

They are designed to walk intimately together – prayer, praise and worship. They are POWER producers on the inside of you.

It is impossible to talk about praise and worship without talking about King David. He was a skilled harp and flute player, psalmist, prophetic scribe, warrior, and worship arts leader who knew how to earnestly seek, find and wait on the Lord. We can learn so much from his ministry concerning how to present our "ministry gifts" in excellence of spirit to Father.

David understood the power of individual and corporate praise and worship. He was bold enough to praise and worship God alone as well as in a corporate setting because *his heart* desired to glorify God for his sovereignty in and through his life. He knew that when pure praise forth, an open heaven was presented before him will God was excited live, dwell and move among men. David also knew that praise increased his faith and confidence in God, and numerous times in his life God brought great victories over seemingly impossible circumstances as a result.

Ministry requires POWER, dominion and authority. Prayer, praise and worship gives us access to Father's power and will for us. Here are some additional examples of what happens in the midst of praise:

1. **Praise is very important to God.** The bible tells us that we were created for God's pleasure to praise. **(Isaiah 43:21; Ephesians 1:12)**

2. **When prophets approached the Tabernacle to prophesy, they were often accompanied by praise and worshippers.** *1 Samuel 10:5 says, "After that you shall come to the hill of God where*

the Philistine garrison is. And it will happen, when you have come there to the city, that you will meet a group of prophets coming down from the high place with a stringed instrument, a tambourine, a flute, and a harp before them; and they will be prophesying."

3. **When we greet brethren the bible says we should do so with praise. Ephesians 5:18-20** says, *"...be filled with the Spirit. Speak to one another with psalms, hymns and spiritual songs. Sing and make music in your heart to the Lord, always giving thanks to God the Father for everything, in the name of our Lord Jesus Christ."*

4. **When we teach and counsel one another we should do so with praise. Colossians 3:16** says, *"Let the word of Christ dwell in you richly as you teach and counsel one another with all wisdom, and as you sing psalms, hymns and spiritual songs with gratitude in your hearts to God."*

5. **Praise sets the atmosphere for the spirit of prophecy to come forth.** *"But now bring me a musician. Then it happened, when the musician played, that the hand of the LORD came upon him."* **2 Kings 3:15**

6. **Music was set aside in the Tabernacle specifically to set the atmosphere for prophesy to come forth.** *"David, together with the commanders of the army, set apart some of the sons of Asaph, Heman and Jeduthun for the ministry of prophesying, accompanied by harps, lyres and cymbals."* **1 Chronicles 25:1**

7. **The ministers didn't just put <u>anyone</u> up in front of the people to praise and worship God, but they chose those who were skillful at it. God wants a perfect praise – one from the heart and from man's desire to honor God with his best.** *"Chenaniah, the head Levite was in charge of the singing; that was his responsibility because he was skillful at it."* **--1 Chronicles 15:22**

8. **God has preserved and saved us so we can praise him.** *"Save us, O LORD our God, And gather us from among the Gentiles, To give thanks to Your holy name, To triumph in Your praise."* **Psalm 106:47**

When you feel the urgency to recite your poem behind *original music inspired* by God, it's not just something you want to do. It is actually Holy Spirit drawing you into setting an atmosphere in which he can dwell and flow through you in power. **This is why we can't take things out of the world and bring them into the sanctuary.** Please hear me when I say this: God cannot dwell inside something created by the adversary. Praise and worship is SACRED to God. It's sacrificial. It's an offering. Now, when people hear the words he has spoken through you the power of God will be upon them even greater because they were birth in worship and in praise to Abba Father.

Tainted praise and worship is an abomination to our Father. How dare his prophetic scribes put something birth out of the world under or above the words he released from the throne room and then call what he created holy or anointed. Our Father abides in the praises of *his* people. If God is not there, then you must ask this question, "Who is abiding in those praises … me or the adversary?"

Who Wrote the Psalms? David did not write all of the psalms in the bible. There are eight known authors identified in the scriptures. The authors of the remaining books are unknown.	
David	Believed to have written at least 73 psalms. Other psalms by David appear in other books.
Asaph	Director of Music during the reign of King David and King Solomon. Believed to have written 12 psalms.
Sons of Korah	Levites serving in the Temple wrote 12 psalms.
King Solomon	Believed to have written at least two of the psalms. He is said to have written more, but they were not included in the bible.
Moses	Credited with writing Psalm 90.
Hemen	Psalmist who worked with King David and Asaph who is credited with writing Psalm 88.
Ethan	Temple worshipper who wrote Psalm 89.
Ezra	Credited with writing Psalm 119, the longest psalm in the bible.
Anonymous	The remaining psalms have unknown authors.

A Scribal Secret Revealed in the Midst of Praise Worship

David experienced the POWER behind praise and worship. By power, I am specifically speaking of the anointing – the destroying of yokes and the breaking of bondages. He saw it remove the enemies' hands in the life of King Saul, he saw praise cause God to move in the midst of men in battle, he saw it break great sorrows in his own life and bring him into a place of peace and joy. I was through these experiences that he is teaching us to push through every situation and circumstance to seek refuge in the face of God. **It was in the place that David is showing us how to tap into a sacred scribal secret.**

Every prophetic literary work begins with a flood of revelation and insight released from the spiri realm. Once we receive that revelation, Father cultivates it and only then can we transcribe wha we receive.

Psalm 86:1-3 says: *"Bow down your ear, O Lord, hear me; For I am poor and needy. Preserve my life, fo I am holy; You are my God; Save your servant who trusts in you! Be merciful to me, O Lord, For I cry to you all day long."*

In many instances David was not overshadowed by the Holy Spirit to the point of inspiration when he began the process of writing. Instead, we see him approaching the Father in humility and earnestness with a heavy heart seeking forgiveness and/or refuge. Because the passion of the scribe and his posture of prayer, it was a supernatural response to his pain for him to reach for his pen and paper to write what was on his heart.

This was David's response to everything.

David had a secret. It was journaling his way into prayer, praise and worship for healing and deliverance. He went to God with the very gifts Father had deposited inside him. I pray you are hearing this in the spirit. David didn't turn to something that was unfamiliar to him. He didn't run to people. Instead, he reached for the very weapon that had been birth in his spirit to fight his internal and external battles – the Scribal Anointing that was upon his life.

For me, I often wrote in the midst of my pain, confusion and frustration. Like David, I'd start our angry or in confusion and before long, I'd end up singing the praises of the Lord. While this type of writing is therapeutic verses prophetic, it is still the work of Holy Spirit. You see, one of the roles Holy Spirit has in your life is to expose sin and push you into a place of conviction of that sin. For the prophetic scribe, he will use your own gift to get you to confess your sin before the Lord – so that liberty and freedom can come into your soul.

Journaling, by definition, is a writing technique that can be used to reduce stress caused by strenuous events in a person's life. It is a safe place to release things that one might otherwise not be able to utter. Prophetic writers often describe journaling as an opportunity to converse with God without speaking. It is in the journal that they cry, shout, scream, laugh and find their way back into the arms of the Father. While David is clearly not the role model Father has set forth for the scribe, his ministry uncovers how *The Scribal Anointing*® can be used to initiate spiritual healing.

Psalm 3:1-4 says:
"LORD, how they have increased who trouble me!
Many are they who rise up against me.
Many are they who say of me,
There is no help for him in God.

But You, O LORD, are a shield for me,
My glory and the One who lifts up my head.
I cried to the LORD with my voice,
And He heard me from His holy hill."

Psalm 3:1-2 shows David crying out to the Lord for the predicament that he's in. **Psalm 3:3-4** shows him entering a place of praise and exaltation to God. This is important. When pure praise and worship comes forth, the presence of God enters and those burdens are lifted; people become pregnant with vision and purpose; prophecy comes forth, plans and instructions are revealed; strategy is uncovered; and birthing takes place.

You see, if we are obedient and begin to write in sincerity and truth – the Holy Spirit will take control. Just as you exercise to remain physically fit in this natural body, you must also exercise the gifts that are within you. It may not be the type of exercise we envision, but it is exactly what our Father has in mind. Scribes of the King, don't neglect the power of journaling.

UNLEASHING THE SCRIBAL ANOINTING WITHIN

If you have combed every inch of this book, I am assured that you have all the information and tools you need to begin walking in an uncompromising scribal ministry. In fact, if you were guided by the Spirit in your reading… that transformation has probably already begun. The question isn't really whether or not this book is going to lead or guide you to a certain level or place in God. Rather, it is whether or not you are willing to continue to follow the Spirit and obtain deep counsel concerning YOUR HEART.

Many prophetic scribes and prophetic writers have come to me saying:

- No one recognizes my gifting;
- I am not used in my local church;
- No one takes me seriously;
- I'm looked at as a joke by my peers;
- I have no outlet to minister, or
- I can't find anyone else to talk to who know how I feel.

Let me tell you, my heart cries out for those who seem to be stuck in the places of above and who are not clear concerning what do or how to obtain direction. I do, however, want you to consider something very, very important: *It's time to let go of those offenses – whether they are things you perceive to be true or whether you have actually been wronged.*

I've learned that if there is offense in my heart, it means that there is some area of pride that I have to let go. It's a sign that I need to "die" some more, so that Christ and his work in me can be fulfilled.

Are you ready to do that? Please understand that you can't wait for man to validate your ministry! You can't wait for man to recognize you or put you to work! You can only trust and depend on what God has revealed and allow Holy Spirit to guide you every step of the way.

Sometimes, my brothers and sisters, we are our own worst enemy. We let our past mistakes, the words we hear, the reactions we receive and the thoughts of others dictate who we are and where we are going in our lives. I have met people who pattern their entire lives chasing after prophecy, and getting angry with the prophet because the word has not come to pass. If God has promised you something, all you can do is stay on the obedient path he has set for you and you will MEET your destiny. Just learn obedience! We've all struggled in this area – especially with the pull that we sometimes face from the world. The greater your calling, the more difficult the struggle may be. Many prophetic scribes who are bursting at the seams to release their gifts are waiting on a pastor or a worship arts leader to recognize or release them.

They are so preoccupied by their pastor's response that they miss God. I'm not saying run outside the protocols of your leadership and go do whatever you want to do. I am saying step back and ALLOW GOD to have His way. Don't be preoccupied by that lack of response. Just move as the Lord tells you to move. Sometimes, God wants to get all of the stuff out of us first before we are positioned in certain arenas. Just waiting on Father to move in situations like this is teaching and training!

I'm speaking to you from my heart here. It is a terrible thing to move AHEAD of yourself in ministry. As Paul told Timothy, "Don't wreck your ship. Slow down... "

Lord, I pray this is making sense to those who read this. My mentor once told me, "*If you are in place or position where you cannot teach, then God is telling you that you need to be learning. If you are in a place or position where you can teach, then you need to make sure that understanding comes forth.*"

Many believers have warped the purpose of the church in their minds. As a result, some have come to believe – within their own intellect – that their gifts must be used in and validated by the church and its leadership. This is not always the case.

Perhaps what you want to do does not fit the vision or purpose of that church or congregation at that time. Perhaps the Lord has not given that pastor a heart for what you want to do just yet or brought the proper training in that area. That does not make the pastor or the leadership wrong, it may mean that they are focused in another area that the Lord has them right now. Instead of becoming offended and frustrated, line up with the ministry focus.

If you were in a university setting attending classes, more than likely you would never insist that your professor use your gift or talent before the class. The local church is Father's chosen institution of learning in the Kingdom of Heaven. Shouldn't your posture then be one of a student and servant?

The word says plainly that your gifts will make room for you. It does not say your church or your leadership will make room for you. So I beg you: "Don't get angry with the pastor! Don't get angry with me for sharing this with you. Simply learn to see God and seek Him in everything."

We must realize that our Father is raising a standard in the literary ministry right now. This year he is positioning and establishing us. He is raising awareness in the body of Christ concerning our role and purpose, and sending people who already have this understanding to teach and impart in others. If we are out of position, then who will till the ground for those to come? *I ask you today who will sacrifice their desires and go for them?*

It is graduation time! We have been commanded *"to use whatever gift we have received to serve others, faithfully administering God's grace in its various forms."* ~ **1 Peter 4:10**

I know it is difficult sometimes to push beyond the hindrances, especially when you have been ignored, intentionally overlooked, outright embarrassed and mocked before men in the very places where you should have been celebrated. This may sound cruel but, get over it! This is just another day in the Kingdom of Heaven. If they mocked the Christ, how much more will they mock you who are not the Christ!

When the world mistreated and rejected Paul and Silas and threw them in prison, they did not sit there and say, *"Well, I'll just do my time and then do what God said do."* They knew that if they had given up they would die without ever fulfilling their ministry. They never said let us just sit and wait until our Father saves us. Instead, they were so fixed on finishing the task at hand that they picked up the tools of warfare – praise and worship – and went into Holy Ghost praise. The Holy Spirit descended in the midst, and instantly the doors of the jail broke free, the shackles that had them bound fell off and they walked out of that prison with a testimony and souls were saved.

"And when they had laid many stripes on them, they threw them into prison, commanding the jailer to keep them securely. Having received such a charge, he put them into the inner prison and fastened their feet in the stocks. But at midnight Paul and Silas were praying and singing hymns to God, and the prisoners were listening to them. Suddenly there was a great earthquake, so that the foundations of the prison were shaken; and immediately all the doors were opened and everyone's chains were loosed." **– Acts 16:23-26**

Endure the STORM until the doors are opened and the chains are loosed! *The Scribal Anointing®* has been unleashed! It's time to praise him! It's time to answer the call! It's time to covet to prophesy with your inkhorn and battle axe! To be unleashed means to be set free from any form of restraint. Be free to be who Father called you to be!

The Next Step

You are not alone in your walk in building a pure scribal ministry based solely on the word of God and not the opinions of men. God is always with you, and the Voices of Christ family has been commissioned to nurture, equip and build an army of Holy Spirit filled present day scribes who are not ashamed of the Gospel of Jesus Christ. It is truly a blessing that you have been chosen to war with pens and notebooks for such a time as this. Thank you, for seeing God in the midst of us and embracing this teaching.

Pray this prayer with me today:

> Father, *I come in the name of your son Jesus Christ,* and I thank you for choosing me as a present day scribe to proclaim your prophetic creative word to the nations. I honor you Father for your mercy, goodness and grace. I come to you now, and repenting for taking ownership of the ministry and the gifts you have placed inside me. I repent for defining who I am by man's standards and for not seeking you fervently to understand who I am in Christ Jesus.

I repent for taking up my plans and desires for my life and overlooking yours. Right now, in the name of Jesus, I lay down my will for my life and I ask for divine instructions and guidance concerning your will for me.

I desire to come in the name of the book that was written for me. I desire to walk out the thoughts and plans that you have for me – thoughts that are good, that are of hope and a future in you. Teach me your ways Father, show me your paths. Lead me into all truths.

I repent for using everything that you have entrusted to me for my glory and for selfish gain. I renounce the spirit of entertainment on my life, the lives of my family members even through the generations. I repent for walking in a spirit of entertainment instead of a spirit of service unto you. I repent for seeking to please man. I repent for allowing people to make me an idol. I repent for turning my gift into an idol and worshiping it. Purge my spirit and my soul of those things that defile me and block my ability to hear your voice. Purge my spirit of those things I've learned in the world that prevents my spirit from clearly hearing your voice. Unlock my spirit which has been closed in some areas and revive my heart before you. Make me teachable Oh Lord. Teach me, Holy Spirit t to submit to your authority in my life. I give you permission, Holy Spirit, to renovate my mind that I may have the mind of Christ, and that my thoughts will be on Jesus continuously.

Today, I release the old and walk into the new. Lord, I reclaim my position in the body of Christ as a ready writer walking under the Scribal Anointing. I denounce every demonic stronghold on my life that carried over from the scribes of old. I denounce pride, arrogance, religion, self-righteousness, the spirit of vipers, hypocrisy and cunning, control, manipulation and all other associated spiritual strongholds. I decree and declare that today I walk in humility, submission, and love in Jesus name.

I forgive all those who have hurt me by minimizing my role in the Kingdom and mocking the ministry you have placed inside me. I forgive my loved ones, church leaderships, friends, coworkers and all others who have hurt me. Now forgive me Father for the anger and bitterness I have harbored in my heart against them. Forgive me for the things that I said. I cause a crop failure, in the name of Jesus, to every word that has gone out from my mouth and from the mouth of my adversaries that was intended for evil. I tear down and uproot every negative word, prayer, prophecy and declaration that has been spoken over me, my loved ones, my church family and any others associated to me that does not line up with your word. Father, I ask that you bless those who have cursed me and wrongfully misused me, and make their way prosperous before you.

Consecrate me, so that I may be used for your glory and your glory alone. Give me wisdom and the supernatural ability to understand your word. Increase my discernment oh Father in heaven. Touch my lips with hot coals that I may speak only the words that you place in my mouth. Anoint my hands to war with my pen and pencil, keyboard and mouth that you, and you alone, may be glorified. Make my path narrow and set me on the road called strait. Let the words of my mouth and the meditation of my heart stand holy and acceptable in your sight.

Give me a hunger and a thirst for your word like never before. Teach me to pray Father so that I can receive answers. Teach me to worship and praise you like never before. Crush my heart. Bend me into your will Father. I decree that a spirit of deliverance and healing will come over me, and that all whom I come in contact with will receive Christ. I break every spirit of slothfulness and procrastination off of my life and the life of my family for generations. I decree that this year I will complete every project that you have set before to complete. I decree that I will be accountable to myself heavenly father and to those whom you have placed in authority and in divine relationship with me.

Align me with Christ-minded believers. Renovate my relationships and knit me with the men and women of God you desire that I be in fellowship with. Open my ears that I may receive your preached word, and teach me not to forsake the fellowship of brethren. Lord, use me. Empty me, that I may be an asset to the Kingdom of Heaven and not a liability to the body of Christ.

I decree before the heavens and the earth that I will walk in present truth. I decree that my choices will be based on your word and not my will. I decree today that I am not the owner of me, but you are Father. I decree that from this moment forward I am a like scribe instructed in the Kingdom of Heaven who is the master of his house and who releases treasures from his royal storehouse of things new and old, and from the ancient of days. I decree that I am a prophetic creative mouth piece of God. Have your way in my life. I seal this prayer under the blood of Jesus.

In Jesus' name I pray. Amen

BIBLIOGRAPHY

Davies, Philip R., *Scribes and Schools: The Canonization of the Hebrew Scriptures*, Kentucky: Westminster John Knox Press, 1998.

Easton, M.G, M.A., D.D., *Illustrated Bible Dictionary*, Third Edition, Thomas Nelson, 1897. Public Domain, http://www.jewishencyclopedia.com/.

Elwell, Walter A. and Comfort, Philip Wesley, *Tyndale Bible Dictionary*, Illinois: Tyndale House Publishers, 2008.

Heszer, Catherine, *Jewish Literacy in Roman Palestine*, Tubingen: 2001, 480.

Keith, Chris, *Jesus AGAINST the Scribal Elite*, Baker Academic, Grand Rapids: 2014.

Orr, James. "Entry for Ezra," *International Standard Bible Encyclopedia*, 1915.

Sukenik, E.L., Ancient Synagogues in Palestine and Greece (1934), 57-61; M. Avi-Yonah, Views of the Biblical World, Vol. V (1961), 63.

Whiston, William. Translator. *"The Works of Josephus,"* Peabody: Hendrickson Publishers, 2004.

OTHER BOOK RECOMMENDATIONS

Pharisees, Scribes & Sadducees in Palestinian Society by Anthony Saldarini

Jewish Literacy: The Most Important Things to Know About Jewish Religion, It's People, and Its History by Rabbi Joseph Telushkin

Jewish Historical Treasures by Azriel Eisenburg

The Essential Talmud by Adin Steinsaltz

Manners & Customs in the Bible: An Illustrated Guide to Daily Life in Biblical Times by Victor H. Matthews

Scribes, Visionaries and the Politics of the Second Temple Judea by Richard A. Horsely

Twentieth Century Encyclopedia of Religious Knowledge by Koeberle-Zwischen

Jesus AGAINST the Scribal Elite by Chris Keith

Scribal Culture & The Making of the Hebrew Bible by Karel van der Toorn

TEACH THE SCRIBAL ANOINTING®

Learn more about becoming a certified instructor of The Scribal Anointing curriculum while moving through intense mentorship. For more information, visit the Apostolic Prophetic School of the Scribe, schoolofthescribe.com, to download a current Certificate to Teach The Scribal Anointing Application Packet.

OTHER OPPORTUNITIES TO LEARN

Numerous courses are offered through the Voices of Christ Apostolic-Prophetic School of the Scribe, schoolofthescribe.com, for those interested in learning more about scribal ministry. Other scribe schools are held through the following events:

- The Apostolic-Prophetic Scribal Advance, a two to four-day intensive scribal gathering;

- Scribes Over This City, a one-day introduction to the ministry of the prophetic scribe held in cities across the United States in collaboration with other ministers, organizations, businesses or ministries; and

We also offer other initiatives and opportunities to learn in an exclusive community of believers. For more information about our private ministry encounters specifically for pastors of churches, celebrities (meaning high profile ministers), etc. Please contact Theresa Harvard Johnson directly through the email provided on the next page.

MEET THERESA HARVARD JOHNSON

Theresa Harvard Johnson is best known for her revelatory insight, understanding and apostolic teachings surrounding the ministry of the prophetic scribe and prophetic writing. She has published, contributed to or co-authored more than 14 books including her signature publication, *"The Scribal Anointing: Scribes Instructed in the Kingdom of Heaven,"* which has been taught world-wide. Walking under a heavy apostolic mandate, Theresa has an intense desire to see the ministry of the prophetic scribe fully restored within the congregation, particularly as it relates to those scribes destined to lead at a global capacity, especially those intricately positioned in government, education, worship and the arts. At the heart of this call is a *fiery and fierce* passion to see every believer come to know, understand and embrace this high calling upon their lives and within the communities they impact.

Available Books:

Identifying & Releasing Chaotic People
Writing & the Prophetic
The Scribal Realm of Dreams & Visions
The Scribal Realm Companion (Dream & Impact Journal)
The Scribal Anointing: Scribes Instructed in the Kingdom of Heaven
The Scribal Companion Student Workbook
Scribal Purpose: 10 Reasons Why God Has Called You to Write
The Sin of Spiritual Critiquing Literary Works
Literary Evangelism Beyond The Open Mic
The Sin of Spiritual Plagiarism: Unauthorized Vessels
40 Signs of a Prophetic Scribe
Signs of a Scribal Prophet
50 Indisputable Biblical Facts About the Ministry of the Prophetic Scribe

*Books are available on Amazon.com & The Book Patch.

Email: scribes@schoolofthescribe.com
Resource Center: voicesofchrist.com
School: schoolofthescribe.com

CPSIA information can be obtained
at www.ICGtesting.com
Printed in the USA
LVHW061824130720
660549LV00007B/560

9 781535 082228